THE CASE FOR
SHAREHOLDER
CAPITALISM

HOW THE PURSUIT OF PROFIT
BENEFITS ALL

THE CASE FOR

SHAREHOLDER CAPITALISM

HOW THE PURSUIT OF PROFIT BENEFITS ALL

R. DAVID McLEAN

Print ISBN: 978-1-952223-88-4
eBook ISBN: 978-1-952223-89-1

Cover design: Jon Meyers

Printed in the United States.

CATO INSTITUTE
1000 Massachusetts Ave. NW
Washington, DC 20001
www.cato.org

For Ethan and Evelyn and their generation

TABLE OF CONTENTS

Part One: Shareholder Capitalism in the Grand Scheme of Things

Part Two: Common Fallacies

Part Three: A Closer Look at Corporate
Social Responsibility

INTRODUCTION

Nobody ever saw a dog make a fair and deliberate exchange of one bone for another with another dog. Nobody ever saw one animal by its gestures and natural cries signify to another, this is mine, that yours; I am willing to give this for that.[1]

—*Adam Smith*

Let's start at the beginning—East Africa, 320,000 years ago. In a series of studies published in the journal *Science*, researchers describe archaeological evidence from this era of early humans producing sophisticated tools and dyes.[2] There was a jump in the sophistication of the tools compared with those from earlier periods. Some of the tools were made from black obsidian, a volcanic glass that can be easily shaped into sharp objects. It is still used today to make some surgical scalpels. But the nearest source of obsidian was more than 50 miles away. Researchers also found black pigments or "paleo-crayons." These pigments had to have been formed in a briny lake, but the nearest body of water that could have produced them was 18 miles away. The totality of the evidence led the researchers to conclude that there had been long-distance trade networks. This conclusion built on earlier research that provided evidence of trade networks in East Africa as early as 200,000 years ago.[3]

About 40,000 years ago, some humans arrived in Europe. Our cousins, the Neanderthals, had been comfortably living in Europe for 200,000 years or so before the first *Homo sapiens* showed up. The Neanderthals then disappeared 10,000 years later. The Neanderthals were physically stronger than us and better adapted to the harsh European winters of that time. Yet we survived, and they went extinct. What happened?

One study concludes that we outcompeted Neanderthals because we traded and they did not.[4] Why would trading help us survive? Trade enables specialization. The researchers reasoned that some people may be good at hunting, while others are better at making clothes and tools. People can then specialize and become either hunters or craftsmen. The community then produces both more meat and more clothes and tools that are of higher quality. Everyone is better off. Fertility increases. The population grows. So even though our biology put us at a disadvantage, trade and specialization may have ensured our survival.

About 12,000 years ago, some people stopped living as hunter-gatherers and focused on farming. This change led to towns and then cities. One of the first cities was Uruk, established 6,500 years ago in Mesopotamia, site of modern-day Iraq.[5] In its prime, Uruk may have had over 60,000 residents.[6] The earliest evidence of writing is 5,500 years old and comes from Uruk.[7] What do you think these ancient city dwellers wrote about? Love? War? Peace? No, they wrote accounting entries to keep track of quantities of grain and other goods. Cities are centers of commerce. Writing first came about to enable large-scale trading.

Writing led to written legal codes. The Code of Hammurabi is the best preserved of the ancient legal codes. It was issued by King Hammurabi, who ruled the Old Babylonian Empire 3,773 years ago. A copy of Hammurabi's Code from that era, etched in stone and seven feet tall, is on display in the Louvre Museum in Paris. Many of its 282 rules pertain to trade. There was a good deal of specialization in Hammurabi's kingdom, and many of the rules governed various professions. King Hammurabi had a keen interest in product quality. Rule 229 states: "If a builder builds a house for someone, and does not construct it properly, and the house which he built falls in and kills its owner, then that builder shall be put to death." If you think that is bad, Rule 230 states: "If it kills the son of the owner, the son of that builder shall be put to death."

About 250 years ago, Adam Smith, a Scottish philosopher who lived with his mother, wrote about the importance of trade. Smith published *The Wealth of Nations*, which is considered the beginning of modern economics.[8] Trade during Smith's time involved the exchange of goods and services for money, as opposed to bartering, which had been common in earlier times. People during Smith's time saw money as wealth and concluded that the seller benefited more from trading. There were restrictions on trade to prevent money from leaving countries and even localities. Smith argued against those restrictions. He recognized that both sides benefit from trade, not just the seller. When two parties trade, each gives up something that it values less, in exchange for something that it values more. That is why the trade happens; there is a mutual benefit.

Smith recognized that trade enables specialization. He used pin-making to demonstrate the power of specialization. Smith reasoned that it is unlikely that a single person could make a single pin in a day, even if the necessary metal, which had to be created by a special process, was available. During Smith's time, 10 people in a pin factory could produce 48,000 pins in a day. Each person focused on a single task. One drew out the wire, one straightened the wire, one cut the wire, one created the point, another created the head, and so on.

The Wealth of Nations explains how trade, specialization, and investment combine to create a productive cycle. The pin maker can sell his pins, pay his bills, buy what he needs, and still have something left over. This surplus can be invested back into the pin-making business, perhaps paying for more sophisticated tools and equipment, to make pins even more efficiently, which in turn creates even larger surpluses. This is not a bad description of how an economy grows, a topic that we will give some attention to in this book.

Smith wrote about the importance of property rights, which promote free trade and specialization. Property rights mean that a person or organization has ownership and exclusive use of a resource. An owner has the right to earn income from the resource and to sell the resource. Property rights prohibit stealing and government expropriation. Government can play an important role in promoting free trade by enforcing property rights. Property rights create the incentive to accumulate wealth and invest, which in turn creates more goods, services, and mutually beneficial trading. What's the point of saving and investing if everything can be taken from you?

Free trade and property rights are the main components of capitalism. The word "capitalism" was originally a pejorative invented by 19th-century socialists. Capitalism is not a philosophy. The term "capitalism" describes a society in which people trade freely and respect property rights. Put differently, in a capitalist economy, we keep trading with one another as we have been for thousands of years, and the government enforces property rights, which encourages even more trade.

This brings us to the topic of this book. Shareholder capitalism is based on the idea that mutually beneficial trading, coupled with property rights, applies to business owners. A business is a person or group of persons who specialize in creating and trading a good or service. In modern times, business owners can use various legal structures to operate their businesses, including sole proprietorships, partnerships, limited liability companies, and corporations. If a corporation is formed, the business owners are issued shares that enable them to control the corporation. The business owners are then referred to as "shareholders."

Some corporations are small businesses that have a single shareholder. In contrast, a publicly traded corporation that has its shares traded on a stock exchange can have millions of shareholders located all over the world. The division of ownership into millions of shares makes it easier for firms to raise capital. It also creates a wide separation between ownership and control. The shareholders own the business, but they cannot collectively control its operations.

Shareholder capitalism speaks to the responsibilities of the persons who manage a corporation on behalf of the shareholders. The one thing that all shareholders have in common is that they prefer more wealth to less. Thus, the corporate manager's job is to create wealth for the corporation's shareholders. Just as a customer would not buy a product from a business unless she stood to benefit from the purchase, so too a corporate manager should not enter into transactions with customers, or any other party, unless the shareholders benefit. Corporate managers should not use the firm's assets for purposes that do not benefit the shareholders. That is the essence of shareholder capitalism.

Here is another way to see it. Customers, suppliers, and employees all freely choose whether to trade with a corporation or not. Customers decide whether they want to buy its products. Employees decide whether they want to sell the corporation their labor. Suppliers decide whether they want to sell it their goods and services. Each of these parties only chooses to trade if it expects to gain from the transaction. No one is forced to do anything. When these parties trade with a corporation, they are trading with its shareholders.

In publicly traded corporations, the shareholders don't operate the business, so they don't get to decide if potential trades benefit them. They hire professional managers for that. Therefore, the corporate manager's job is to ensure that the firm's trades benefit the shareholders. Otherwise, the firm's trading is not mutually beneficial, and in that case, why would anyone want to be a shareholder?

It's important not to get confused by the terms "corporation" and "shareholders." The corporation is a legal entity; it exists only on paper and in our imaginations. The corporation is essentially a set of rules regulating how people trade with a business, how the business is taxed, and how it is governed. Employees, suppliers, and customers trade with the shareholders—that is, the business owners—through a set of rules that make up what we call the corporation. This is also the case with sole proprietorships, partnerships, and limited liability companies, except that the business owners are not called shareholders. In the end, regardless of the names and rules, it is always just people trading with other people, as we have done for millennia.

Controversy and Questions

Shareholder capitalism is often attributed to a famous 1970 *New York Times Magazine* article by the Nobel Prize–winning economist Milton Friedman.[9] Yet Friedman was not proposing a new theory. He was writing in a magazine, not an academic journal. His article was a response to the argument—then growing in popularity—that in addition to creating wealth for shareholders, corporations also have a social responsibility to advance a variety of goals unrelated to maximizing shareholder value.[10]

Friedman argued that professional business managers are employees who work for the business's owners. Employees ought to work for their employer's benefit, not some other objective. Friedman argued that the business and its assets belong to the shareholders, not to the CEO, and not to some vaguely defined notion of society or the common good. This was not a new idea.

Two hundred years earlier, Adam Smith recognized that business owners operate their businesses for their own benefit—and make society better off in the process.

Friedman wrote that the purpose of a business "is to increase its profits." Many took this to mean that the purpose of a business is to maximize short-term profits. Yet the goal is to maximize the value of the business or shareholder wealth. The more valuable the business, the greater the shareholders' wealth. As we will see later in this book, the distinction between short-term profits and business value is important because a manager who is trying to maximize a business's value behaves differently than a manager who is trying to maximize its short-term profits.

Shareholder capitalism is the overarching theme in university finance courses. We teach it in Finance 101. I never thought that Finance 101 was controversial. Yet shareholder capitalism is increasingly under attack. It was under attack in 1970, when Friedman wrote his famous article, but over the past decade, there has been a noticeable surge in hostility. The critics are numerous and influential. They include people in business, politics, media, and academia. The World Economic Forum (WEF) and its founder, Klaus Schwab, are major critics. The WEF's annual meeting in Davos, Switzerland, brings together global leaders in business, politics, and media, and promotes the idea that shareholder capitalism is harmful and needs to be replaced. The Business Roundtable, an association of CEOs from some of America's largest corporations, recently stated that creating wealth for shareholders should not be the corporation's primary goal. The world's largest asset manager, BlackRock, and its CEO, Larry Fink, pressure firms to pursue various social responsibility objectives. Business schools increasingly offer classes that are critical of shareholder capitalism and promote various social responsibility doctrines.

I wrote this book because both shareholder capitalism and the various corporate social responsibility doctrines that are trying to replace it are being misrepresented. This book is my attempt to set the record straight.[11] It is divided into three sections. The first section describes what shareholder capitalism is and what it is not. I give a lot of attention to how shareholder capitalism impacts *non-shareholders*. If businesses are run with the goal of maximizing shareholder value, what are the ramifications for other stakeholders, such as employees, customers, and suppliers? The second section deals with the major criticisms of shareholder capitalism. What are they? Are they valid? The third section examines corporate social responsibility, which encompasses the newer idioms, such as environmental, social, and governance (ESG); stakeholder capitalism; and sustainability. What does it mean for a corporation to be socially responsible? What effect does the pursuit of corporate social responsibility have on shareholders and the rest of society?

Here are some more specific questions that this book will address. How does a firm operate if its goal is to create wealth for its owners? Profits are important. But what is a profit? Does it represent the shareholders winning and other parties losing? Do only short-term profits matter, or do long-run profits matter too? How should a firm treat its other stakeholders, such as customers, suppliers, and employees, if the goal is to maximize shareholder value?

Society has scarce resources that have alternative uses. If we use a resource for one end, we cannot use it for another. How do we best use our scarce resources? Should we make more airplanes and fewer cars? More apartments and fewer houses? What types of drugs should we develop? Should drugs be developed by newer companies, such as Moderna, or more established companies, such as Pfizer? Who should be in charge of such decisions? How are such decisions made under shareholder capitalism?

An economy can be described as having labor (people), capital (machines and other equipment), and technology. Technology means how well labor and capital interact to create goods and services. Technological innovation means that for a given amount of labor and capital, an economy can create more goods and services than it could before. The economy then grows. A developed economy, like the United States, needs innovation to continue growing. How does shareholder capitalism fit into that picture? Does the goal of maximizing shareholder value encourage or inhibit innovation?

There are two common criticisms of shareholder capitalism. The first is that it ignores the well-being of other stakeholders, such as customers, employees, suppliers, and society at large. The second is that it causes corporate managers to focus on short-term profits, thus causing underinvestment and harming the corporation's long-term viability. Are these criticisms valid? If the corporate manager's goal is to create wealth for shareholders, will the manager focus on short-term profits, underinvest, and ignore the well-being of the other stakeholders?

The critics of shareholder capitalism want to replace it with what they say is a new type of capitalism, where the pursuit of social responsibility is the goal, or at least a goal.[12] This idea sounds nice. Most people like the idea of being socially responsible. The problem is that people can have very different views on what is socially responsible. There is no objective answer to this question. Therefore, a key question is, Who gets to decide what is socially responsible?

Governments set the rules under which firms operate. In the United States, there are more than one million federal regulations, each containing multiple rules.[13] The federal government typically issues thousands of new regulations every year. State and local governments issue regulations as well. In shareholder capitalism, the firm's goal is to create shareholder wealth by engaging in mutually beneficial trading while adhering to these regulations. What role then does corporate social responsibility play? Government regulations ultimately come from elected officials.

Where do the persons issuing corporate social responsibility edicts get their authority from?

A business may take an action that both increases its value and is labeled as being socially responsible or consistent with a principle espoused by the growing ESG movement. A business may take a different action that also increases its value but is labeled as socially irresponsible or inconsistent with ESG principles. Do we need to care about labels and monikers? A typical business increases its value by engaging in mutually beneficial trading with its stakeholders, which include its customers, employees, and suppliers, while following the government's rules and regulations. Why does it matter if someone comes along and subjectively labels some of its actions as responsible and others as irresponsible?

In practice, corporate social responsibility tends to promote causes that progressives favor. I am not arguing that these causes are good or bad, but that they are highly partisan. When the assets of a corporation are used to promote an ideological cause, it is a form of expropriation. For example, it would be illegal if a CEO, for no good business reason, transferred $1 million from the corporation to another business owned by the CEO. Yet if the same CEO transferred $1 million from the corporation to a nonprofit that promotes an ideological cause that the CEO favors, it is not a problem under the guise of corporate social responsibility. Yet the economics of the two transfers are the same. In both cases, shareholder value was reduced by $1 million. Why is one type of transfer illegal, but the other considered OK?

There are important questions regarding how corporate social responsibility affects democracy. Consider environmental issues. Businesses often create negative externalities, an economics term for negative side effects, such as pollution. Businesses also create positive things for society, such as wealth, goods, services, and jobs. There is a tradeoff. If we impose regulations that limit the negatives, we also tend to get fewer of the positives.[14] People often disagree over which level of tradeoff is best.[15] The social responsibility edicts typically encourage firms to reduce environmental externalities more than regulations call for. If successful, those edicts can become de facto regulations—and thereby displace the tradeoff created by government regulation with a new tradeoff based on the edicts. Is this how we want to govern ourselves?

It's important to recognize that critiques of capitalism and efforts to replace or alter it with nonmarket mechanisms are not new. The intellectual class, which largely consists of progressives working in academia, government, media, and at various nonprofits, has been at it for more than two centuries.[16] The pattern is predictable. There is always the claim that capitalism creates problems, that intellectuals have the solutions, and that the solutions require limiting individual choice. We will explore some earlier examples of this and the resulting effects on society in this book.

Part One

SHAREHOLDER CAPITALISM IN THE
GRAND SCHEME OF THINGS

1

WHAT IS A PROFIT?

Profits are perhaps the most misconceived subject in economics.[1]

—*Thomas Sowell*

It's common for people to think that shareholder capitalism is about helping the rich get richer at the expense of everyone else. This is untrue. Any system that benefits a small part of the population at the expense of everyone else should be discarded. In practice, that is the situation that communism created.

The central idea of shareholder capitalism is that the goal of a business is to create wealth for its owners. Why would anyone invest in a business if it made them poorer? A business creates wealth for its owners by generating profits. Critics of shareholder capitalism seem to think that profit is the outcome of a zero-sum game—in other words, the firm's shareholders win while other stakeholders, such as customers, suppliers, and employees, lose. If so, then why do those other stakeholders continue to play the game?

Trading needs to be mutually beneficial; otherwise, people stop trading. Consider your own trading. If you are like most people, you trade with a business or some other institution for your income and then use your income to trade with other businesses for goods and services, such as food, clothing, shelter, a smartphone, and so on. These trades make you better off. Otherwise, you would not continue trading. You cannot expect businesses to keep trading with you unless the trading also makes the businesses' owners better off. Profits reflect the business owner's gain from trading.

Capitalism is characterized by *mutually beneficial exchange*. No one is forced to trade with anyone else. If business owners want to become rich in a capitalist system, they need to create goods, services, and jobs that benefit other people. The more mutually beneficial trading a business engages in, the more wealth it creates for its owners. Most business owners are not rich, though, and most businesses close down within five years of opening.[2] Creating a profitable business is not easy, but when it does happen, it benefits both shareholders and the other stakeholders.

Profit Is a Leftover

Profit is not the outcome of a zero-sum game. Profit is a *leftover* that business owners are entitled to *after they have made the other major stakeholders better off.* The shareholders eat last. To say that a firm's goal is to make a profit is to say that when two parties agree to trade, each side gains something. Profit measures the business owner's gain.

$$\text{Profits} = \text{Revenues} - \text{Costs} - \text{Taxes}$$

Profits are measured as revenues minus costs and taxes. Profits reflect what consumers are willing to pay for a good or service, minus what a business pays to create the good or service. It is the other stakeholders, not the shareholders, who collectively determine whether the firm makes a profit. Stakeholders are free to choose whether they want to trade with the firm or not. If a firm cannot make its stakeholders better off, then the stakeholders will not trade with the firm, and the firm will not generate profits. It's as simple as that.

Firms generate revenues by sales to customers. Customers buy a product if its expected value exceeds its price. Why do people keep buying coffee from Starbucks? It must be that the value they place on a cup of coffee exceeds the price that Starbucks is charging them. This is generally true for any product or service. Customers *choose* to purchase a product or service if it serves *their interest*; that is, if the expected benefit or value from the product or service exceeds the price paid. If customers are disappointed, they don't come back, future revenues are not generated, and there are no more profits or shareholder wealth.

Firms rely on employees to create and sell goods and services. Why does someone choose to work at a particular firm? Like customers, employees trade with a firm if it serves their interest. Put differently, employees choose to work at a firm because what it gives them is better than unemployment or what any other employer offers them. A firm must make its employees better off if it is going to generate profits.

A firm relies on suppliers to create its products and services. Therefore, as with employees and customers, a firm must make its suppliers better off for it to make profits. Starbucks doesn't grow coffee or make cups, and it typically leases the properties where its stores are located. Why do suppliers willingly trade with Starbucks or any other firm? Suppliers are willing to sell a product or service if the sale price exceeds their costs. They are willing to supply if they make a profit.

Firms may borrow from creditors. When creditors lend to a firm, they are willingly entering a contract with the firm, in which the firm receives capital and repays the loan at some later date with interest. The loan makes the lender better off, or it would not have agreed to the loan.

Do you see a pattern here? In a capitalist economy, trade between two parties happens only if each party agrees to it. We are all "free to choose," as Milton Friedman pointed out in his book with that phrase as its title. Stakeholders—customers, employees, and suppliers—choose to trade with a business because it makes them better off.

I am not arguing that a profitable firm makes everyone happy all the time. Some people went to Starbucks, didn't like the coffee, and never went back. People frequently change jobs. Suppliers might find that a relationship with a particular customer is not good for them. That's the nice thing about a market economy. We have variations in goods, services, and jobs, and people with different preferences can find what works best for them. To consistently make a profit, though, a firm needs to have enough stakeholders willing to trade with it.

Therefore, when we say that a firm's goal is to make a profit, we are implicitly saying that the firm must please its stakeholders. Otherwise, the stakeholders will not continue to trade with it, there will be no profits, and the firm will have no value. There is no getting around the fact that to create a profit, a firm must serve the interests of its stakeholders.

Whatever profits are available to business owners come after taxes. Firms pay payroll taxes on behalf of each employee, and income taxes on gross profits. Firms can be taxed by federal, state, and local governments.

Do firms pay their fair share of taxes? The answer to that question is another question: Who gets to decide what is fair? "Fair" is a subjective term. Some people think firms don't pay enough taxes. Other people think firms pay too much in taxes. We will probably never have widespread agreement on what is fair when it comes to corporate taxes. That stated, corporate taxes are determined by the tax code, which was created by people that we elected. That is as close to fair as we can get.

Profit versus Fraud

When we talk about profits in capitalism, we mean wealth created by mutually beneficial trading. Each side understands what it is getting and what it is giving up, and both sides are made better off by the trade. If there is fraud or deception, then the deceived party did not get to freely choose. Instead, it was duped into a trade that was not mutually beneficial. What we have then is fraud—in other words, stealing. Simply ending up with more money by any means is not the same thing as making a profit.

Bernie Madoff made a lot of money, but his actions were not consistent with capitalism. Madoff was cheating people. He lied to his customers about his investment fund's performance and then lied to them again about how he was investing their money. When people invested with Madoff, their wealth was transferred to him. This was stealing, not mutually beneficial trading. For that matter, robbing banks creates wealth for bank robbers, but it's not capitalism. There is no mutual benefit. The robber is better off, but the bank is worse off.

Laws and Regulations

Shareholder capitalism espouses profit making while adhering to laws and regulations. Dealing heroin is profitable, but it's also illegal, and therefore not encouraged by shareholder capitalism. Regulations are often intended to address negative side effects, or "externalities," such as pollution, that firms create during their operations. Households, churches, schools, and anything else that involves human activity create negative externalities as well.

Do businesses face too little or too much regulation? That depends on whom you ask. Unfortunately, the universe has not issued an edict regarding what externalities are allowable and in what quantities. We need to decide that as needed. The U.S. government has issued more than a million regulations, each containing multiple rules, that are meant to limit negative externalities.[3] These regulations almost always create costs for businesses, so, along with fewer negative externalities, we also get less of the positive things that businesses create. We get fewer goods, services, jobs, and wealth. We get a smaller economy.

To give us a better perspective on the regulatory hurdles that businesses face, the *New York Times* ran an article in 2017 about an apple orchard and "5,000 Rules."[4] The 5,000 number is just an estimate. How many rules a business faces from federal regulations and what all those rules say is virtually unknowable. To get an estimate of the rules that a firm must follow, one needs a computer algorithm that can search for keywords within the more than one million federal regulations. The *Times* article estimates that there are 12,000 rules that apple orchards must follow, 9,500 of which were added over the previous decade. Many of those rules apply to other businesses besides orchards. There are 5,000 rules that apply only to orchards. Is that too many rules or too few? I'll let the reader decide. As for shareholder capitalism, it does not say what the rules and regulations should be, only that firms need to obey them.

Losses and the Freedom to Choose

Although firms *seek* to make profits, most fail. A profitable firm is an exception, not the rule. A large publicly traded corporation is an outlier. For every one of those, there are millions of firms that failed and entrepreneurs who lost their investments. More than half of new businesses do not survive five years. Only about a third survive 10 years. The survival rate at 20 years is 20 percent.[5]

Shareholder capitalism assigns both profits *and losses* to the shareholders. If a business can engage in mutually beneficial trading such that profits are created, then the shareholders should enjoy those profits. At the same time, if a firm cannot generate profits but instead creates losses, the shareholders should suffer those losses.

Firms make losses and go out of business because their stakeholders are free to choose. Customers don't have to buy their products. Employees don't have to work for them. Suppliers don't have to supply them. Losses mean that a business could not engage in mutually beneficial trades with each of these parties.

Dealing with a business is therefore very different from dealing with a government. My wife and I send our children to public school. Our neighbors send their children to a private school. Yet our neighbors still face the same rate of local taxation that we do. Our local government did not provide our neighbors with a service that they are happy with, but they still have to pay for that service. If they refuse to pay, the government will take their home.

In contrast, down the street from us, there is a shopping plaza with several stores. Our neighbors don't have to shop at or send money to any of these businesses. If people don't like the goods and services these businesses provide, they can shop elsewhere and there is nothing that any of these businesses can do about it. There is a good deal of turnover among the businesses at this plaza. Making profits is not easy.

2

SHAREHOLDER VALUE AND PROFIT

Finance 101 teaches us that shareholder value is the present value of all future cash flows. This is true in practice, not just theory: many of the world's most valuable companies are priced so high because of their growth opportunities, not their current profits.[1]

—*Alex Edmans*

The idea that the goal of a business is to make profits and create wealth for its owners has led to confusion. Some have interpreted this to mean that the firm's goal is to maximize short-term profits. This is not what is meant, and it's strange that people would interpret it that way. If I were to tell you that the goal of life is to pursue happiness, would you interpret this to mean as living only for today, with no thought about how today's actions impact your future?

When we say that the goal of a business is to generate profits, we are not referring to just short-term profits. We mean *all profits over the life of the business*. If you own a business, you have a claim to all its future profits. Shareholder value, therefore, is a function of all future profits over the firm's life. If an owner wants to sell her business today, shareholder value is what a fair selling price would be.

The intuition for valuing a business is to think of it as a stream of cash flow, which is driven by profits. The firm will make some profit—or loss—this year, next year, the year after that, the year after that, and so on. The firm's value is the *present value of all its expected cash flow*. Shareholder value is just firm value minus the value of any debt. There are some timing and accounting differences between profits and cash flow. Over the long run, though, cash flow is driven by profits.

The term *present value* means that $1 in the future is worth less than $1 today. This is because $1 today can be invested and is therefore worth more than $1 in the future. For our purposes, we don't need to go into the details of computing present value and cash flow.[2] Just know that a firm's value reflects all its expected future profits.

Maximizing shareholder value requires corporate managers to play a long game. Shareholders care about short-term profits, but those are typically only a small part of a firm's value. In practice, long-term profits are more important and constitute a larger part of the pie. I'm not stating anything novel here. Students learn this in Finance 101.

The goal of shareholder value maximization also guides how the corporation treats its stakeholders. Intuitively, all else being equal, which firm do you think will have a higher value: one that has good relations with its customers, suppliers, and employees, or one that neglects its stakeholders and survives day to day?

Short-Term Profits versus Long-Term Profits

To get an idea of the importance of long-term profits for shareholder value, consider Microsoft. If we multiply Microsoft's stock price as of August 11, 2023 ($321.01) by its number of shares outstanding

(7.44 billion), we get a market capitalization of $2.39 trillion. This is the stock market's estimate of Microsoft's shareholder value. Microsoft's most recent annual earnings or net income was $72.7 billion, which is much smaller than its market capitalization.

Why are investors willing to pay $2.39 trillion for a company that earns "only" $72.7 billion? Put differently, why is Microsoft's price 31 times greater than its earnings? Because Microsoft's shareholders own all its future profits. When investors value Microsoft, they incorporate all its expected future cash flow into the calculation. Investors expect that Microsoft will continue making profits for a long time and that its profits will grow. Investors' expectations of Microsoft's *future profits* create its enormous value.

The same is true for all of the world's most valuable companies. Apple has a price-to-earnings ratio of 24—in other words, Apple's market capitalization is 24 times greater than its most recent annual earnings. Google's price-to-earnings ratio is 19. Tesla's is 57. With smaller, younger firms the price-to-earnings ratios can be even greater.

Many young firms have negative profits but are still worth millions or even billions of dollars. That is often the case with initial public offerings (IPOs), whereby companies have their shares listed on a stock exchange for the first time. Table 2.1 provides a few examples of recent IPOs that had negative earnings. The value of these companies is based entirely on investors' expectations of future profits.

Investment Can Increase Firm Value

If business owners did not care about future profits, they would not have created their businesses in the first place. When an entrepreneur launches a business, an investment is required. The entrepreneur has less cash on hand after investing in the business.

Table 2.1
Examples of 2022 IPOs with negative earnings

Name	Market Capitalization ($)	2022 Earnings ($)
Credo Technology	2.14 billion	−22.18 million
Amylyx Pharmaceuticals	1.45 billion	−198.38 million
Prime Medicine	1.14 billion	−121.82 million
Belite Bio	639.27 million	−12.65 million
Acrivon Therapeutics	271.66 million	−31.17 million

Source: A list of all 2022 IPOs can be found at https://stockanalysis.com/ipos/2022/. The market capitalization and earnings data are also from stocksanalysis.com. The market capitalizations are as of August 11, 2023.

An investment is, by definition, giving up something now with the hopes of gaining something greater in the future. It is reasonable for an entrepreneur to invest if a business's future profits are expected to offset the initial investment.

This is as true for large corporations as it is for small businesses. In 2021, Pfizer spent more than $14 billion on research and development (R&D) investments. If Pfizer had not done this, it would have had $14 billion more in profits. It could have just paid the $14 billion to its shareholders with a dividend. But Pfizer can be a more valuable business, and its shareholders made better off, if the $14 billion investment creates future profits that are greater. Fewer profits today can mean more profits in the future. Firms create value this way all the time.

Investments include building a factory, buying equipment, investing in R&D, running marketing campaigns, increasing wages and benefits to retain and incentivize employees, and so on. Each of these investments reduces short-term profits and short-term cash flow. Yet each of these investments may also increase shareholder value, by increasing future profits and cash flow by amounts that more than offset the short-term expenses. To create wealth for shareholders, firms need to find investment opportunities where the long-term profits outweigh the near-term costs.

Again, it is useful to think of a business as a cash flow stream. The present value of the cash flow stream is the value of the firm. The corporate manager's goal is to maximize shareholder value, which means making the present value of the cash flow stream as large as possible. With this in mind, we can analyze whether an investment increases or decreases firm value.

The Net Present Value Rule

In Finance 101, we teach a tool that helps managers evaluate investments. The tool is called the *net present value (NPV) rule*. A positive NPV investment increases firm value, because it makes the present value of the cash flow stream larger. A negative NPV investment reduces firm value, because it makes the present value of the cash flow stream smaller. The NPV rule is to accept all positive NPV projects and reject all negative NPV projects.

The following example shows how the NPV rule works: A firm can invest in an R&D project. The cost of the investment is $1 million. Assume that the cost is realized immediately. The R&D is expected to generate a new product, and the profits from that product will be realized over the next 10 years. The expected cash flow generated by those profits has a present value of $5 million.

- The NPV of the project is $5 million − $1 million = $4 million.
- The NPV is positive, so the firm should take the project.
- The NPV is $4 million, so the firm is worth $4 million more if it takes the project.

Put differently, both the present value of the firm's cash flow stream and shareholder value will increase by $4 million. So, even though the firm's short-term earnings have been made lower by $1 million, which is the cost of the R&D, the firm's value has increased by $4 million. *You can both lower short-term profits and increase firm value. Virtually every investment does so.*

If the goal is to maximize shareholder value, then the manager will accept all positive NPV projects and reject all negative NPV projects.

What does it mean to reject a negative NPV project? The NPV rule implicitly recognizes that shareholders can invest outside of the firm. The present value of a project is estimated using the rate of return that shareholders expect to get if they invest in a different business with a similar risk profile.[3] A negative NPV means that the shareholders could earn a higher return if they invest their capital outside of the company. Thus, the resources that could be used in the project can be put to better use by a different firm.

Simple Heuristics

The NPV rule is a measurement tool. It helps business managers gauge if they are making progress toward the goal of maximizing shareholder value. A business manager can pursue this goal without calculating a company's NPV or even knowing what a present value is. People did so for centuries, long before we began teaching these calculations in business schools. Adam Smith recognized the general idea in his writings more than 200 years ago.

For example, a restaurant owner could decide to undergo an expensive renovation. The owner believes that after the renovation, more people will come to the restaurant, and the restaurant will be able to charge higher prices. The owner hasn't done any formal calculations, but he thinks the investment will make the business more valuable. In another example, an employee asks the restaurant owner for a raise. The owner believes that keeping this employee happy and on the staff is worth it, so he agrees to the raise. In both cases, the owner agrees to the additional expenses because the owner thinks it benefits the business. The owner is practicing shareholder capitalism but without any math.

Shareholder Value in Public Corporations

For publicly traded companies, shareholder value is reflected in the stock price. What if the manager believes that the stock price is inaccurate? Does this change the manager's goal? The short answer is no. Shareholder capitalism does not spell out different duties for managers of public corporations and managers of privately held businesses.

Managers of public corporations can convey their expectations to investors in their corporation's annual and quarterly reports and other legal filings, in press releases to the media, and in meetings with analysts and investors. The U.S. Securities and Exchange Commission requires the managers of public corporations to disclose all information relevant to firm value.[4] Investors then use that information to value the business, which in turn helps determine its stock price.

Shareholder value is based on predictions of the future. Managers may believe that profits will grow at a fast rate over the next several years. Investors may think that profits will grow at a slower rate. In this case, the value that investors come up with will be reflected in the stock price, which will be less than the value that the managers estimate. Is the stock price wrong? Perhaps. Or maybe the managers are too optimistic. In any case, stock prices will reflect what investors believe the firm is worth. That can just as easily be more, as it can be less, than what managers think the firm is worth.

Again, a business's value is the present value of all its expected cash flow. The manager's job is to make that value as large as possible. That rule applies to all types of businesses, including public corporations, private corporations, limited liability corporations, partnerships, and businesses that may not be organized along any of these legal structures.

3

HOW SHOULD SOCIETY USE ITS SCARCE RESOURCES?

By directing that industry in such a manner as its produce may be of the greatest value, he intends only his own gain, and he is in this, as in many other cases, led by an invisible hand to promote an end which was no part of his intention.[1]

—*Adam Smith*

The central problem of any economy is that it has scarce resources with alternative uses. If a piece of land, a raw material, a machine, or a person's labor is used for one purpose, it cannot be used for another. We have to decide how to best use our resources. How do we decide what goods and services to produce? Just as importantly, how do we decide what *not* to produce? What role does shareholder capitalism play in all of this? It turns out that the selfish dictum of creating shareholder wealth leads to using resources to produce what is most valued by society.

Profits Reflect a Beneficial Use of Scarce Resources

In shareholder capitalism, the goal is to maximize shareholder value. Shareholder value reflects all future profits. A firm makes a profit if the value of what it makes exceeds the value of what it uses. Consider a car manufacturer. Let's assume it produces a car for a total cost of $50,000. The manufacturer can sell the same car for $60,000.

- The manufacturer therefore makes a gross profit of $10,000 ($60,000 − $50,000 = $10,000).
- The manufacturer can produce the car for $50,000 because various stakeholders, such as employees and suppliers, are willing to sell their parts and labor such that the total cost of the car is $50,000.
- The car maker can sell the car for $60,000 because its customers place a value on the car that is at least $60,000.
- The $10,000 profit reflects the fact that the car maker uses resources on which society places a relatively low value and creates something on which society places a relatively high value.

Thus, a profit-seeking firm uses resources only if the value of what is created exceeds the value of what is used, leaving society better off. In fact, profit likely understates the value created, as the price consumers pay for a product is usually less than the value that they place on the product. If someone is willing to pay $60,000 for a car, the car is worth at least $60,000 to that person, and probably more. Thus, the best way to know whether, and to what extent, a business contributes to society is its profits.

Losses Reflect a Poor Use of Scarce Resources

Some people get upset when they learn a business has made a large profit. This is backward. People should be happy when firms make profits and upset when firms make losses. Consider how the world would look if firms strived for losses. A firm has a loss if the value of its output is less than the value of what it uses. In this case, the resources that the firm uses are worth more to society than the products it creates.

If the car maker in the previous example spent $50,000 to produce a car that it could only sell for $40,000, it would mean that the resources being used to make the car could be put to better use elsewhere in the economy. Society is made worse off by the car maker making this car. It is better when such businesses close.

Imagine if every firm strived for losses instead of profits. Intellectuals are finally successful and convince everyone that capitalism is evil and that profits are the root of this evil. Some people then point out that the opposite of evil is good, so it must be that losses are good! We elect politicians who make this the law of the land. All firms must generate losses. To create losses, firms take resources that society places a relatively high value on and create goods and services that society places a relatively low value on. How would the world look after a few years of this?

As explained in the previous chapter, a business may generate losses temporarily but still go on to create value and benefit society. Many young firms start out losing money as they invest heavily to develop products that are not yet mature enough to generate revenues. Thus, temporary losses may reflect a good use of resources if they are expected to be offset by greater profits in the future. But if a mature firm or product continues to generate losses, it likely signals that the resources it is using could be put to better use elsewhere.

Can a Business Set Prices?

A business, or any seller, can *ask* for any price it wants, but there may be no buyer. I can ask my employer to pay me $1 million a year, but it is not going to happen. Trade happens only if there is a price that is beneficial to both the buyer and the seller.

In the earlier example of the car, the car manufacturer charged $60,000. The car manufacturer could charge $70,000 instead, but people don't have to buy the car. They can buy a different new car, a used car, or no car at all. The car manufacturer chooses a price that maximizes its profits. That price has to be one that some consumers are willing to pay.

We could also ask why a supplier doesn't charge the car manufacturer twice as much for its parts. The supplier is free to do so, but the car manufacturer is also free to use a different supplier.

It may be that the price that consumers are willing to pay for a car is less than the price at which the car manufacturer can make a profit. In this case, the car manufacturer will stop making cars. This is not uncommon; businesses close for this reason all the time.

Resource Allocation and Opportunity Cost

For every investment, there is an opportunity cost, which is the return we would expect to get from an alternative investment of similar risk. If a car manufacturer builds a new factory, its shareholders pay the cost. The shareholders could use this capital to invest in a different car manufacturer or in a different business. Do these alternative investments offer better returns on investment? If so, the factory should not be built, and the shareholders should invest elsewhere.

Society also benefits when corporate managers consider opportunity costs. When a car manufacturer builds a factory, it consumes resources, such as land, building materials, machinery, and labor. Society might benefit more if these resources were used elsewhere. If a business of similar risk can use the same resources and generate more profits, then society benefits more if it uses the resources.

Resource Allocation and the NPV Rule

In the previous chapter, I introduced the NPV (net present value) rule. We teach the NPV rule in Finance 101. It is a tool that helps corporate managers determine whether an investment will create value for the shareholders. The NPV rule accounts for the fact that every investment has an opportunity cost.

Recall that a positive NPV investment increases firm value and creates shareholder wealth, whereas a negative NPV investment decreases firm value and destroys shareholder wealth. In shareholder capitalism, the rule is to invest in all positive NPV investments and avoid all negative NPV investments.

An investment's NPV is driven by three factors:

1. Cost of the investment
2. Profits that the investment is expected to generate
3. Expected rate of return from alternative investments of similar risk

An NPV essentially answers this question: Are the expected profits from this investment more or less than the expected profits from investing in a different business of similar risk? If more, it is a positive NPV and creates shareholder wealth. If less, it is a negative NPV and destroys shareholder wealth.

When a firm skips a negative NPV investment, it is choosing not to use resources that could be put to better use by a different firm. The corporate manager recognizes that the shareholders have better investment opportunities outside of the firm. Making the investment would be a poor use of society's scarce resources. A negative NPV investment, therefore, not only makes the shareholders poorer but also makes society poorer, as it consumes resources that could have gone to a more valuable use.

As we will see in the second section of this book, some critics of shareholder capitalism seem to think that it is always better for firms to invest more. That perspective overlooks the fact that there is always an opportunity cost. Whenever a firm invests, it uses resources that have an alternative and potentially better use. If a firm can't use resources to create products and services that are part of a positive NPV investment, then it shouldn't use the resources. Leave them be and let someone else use them for a more highly valued purpose.

Shareholders Eat Their Losses

Even the best-intentioned corporate managers make investments that turn out badly. Investments and NPV analyses are based on guesses about the future. The guesses may turn out to be wrong. Demand for a product may be lower than expected. The cost of an investment may be higher than expected. These things happen all the time.

In shareholder capitalism, bad investments are self-correcting. Investors lose money when they invest in a venture that turns out poorly. Although the investment may have been well-intentioned, if in the end it is not a good use of society's resources, the shareholders are made poorer. This is a good thing. It creates incentives to carefully scrutinize how resources are being used and to quickly end unprofitable ventures that are not creating value.

The goal of maximizing shareholder value thus aligns the shareholders' interest with those of the rest of society. Society has a problem. How should it allocate scarce resources? The answer is to use resources only if the products created are more valuable than the resources being used, while accounting for opportunity costs. When business managers pursue the goal of maximizing shareholder value, they do just that. There is no central planner or facilitator, but each resource is put to its best use. Adam Smith, the father of modern economics, recognized this effect more than two centuries ago when he wrote his famous maxim about the invisible hand, which is quoted at the beginning of this chapter.

4

GROWTH AND INNOVATION: THE ROLE OF PROFIT

Economic growth occurs whenever people take resources and rearrange them in ways that make them more valuable.[1]

—*Paul Romer*

A nation's economic growth rate determines its future prosperity. The higher the economic growth rate, the more living standards increase. The size of a nation's economy can be measured by its gross domestic product (GDP). GDP can be estimated as the value of everything that is produced in an economy minus the costs of production. A nation's economic growth can then be measured as growth in *GDP per capita*, which is GDP divided by population. If we want our children and grandchildren to have the highest possible standard of living, then we need to care about economic growth rates.

A nation's voters may prefer the tradeoff of less growth in exchange for the effects of various social and environmental policies. Yet within the confines of whichever policies they choose, faster growth is better. If Sweden, for example, can keep all its social and environmental policies in place and grow at 3 percent per year instead of 2 percent per year, then Swedes will be better off.

The Nobel Prize-winning economist Paul Romer argues that people tend to underestimate the importance of long-run growth rates.[2] We tend to be good at adding things up, but we underestimate how quickly things grow when compounding is involved, which comprises more than just simple addition.

To see the importance of compounding, consider two economies, both with GDP per capita of $10,000. One will grow at 2 percent annually, while the other will grow at 3 percent. This 1 percent difference in annual growth seems small, but it can have an enormous impact on living standards if it persists for a long enough period of time, as shown in Table 4.1.

Table 4.1 displays GDP per capita for two economies at different times over the subsequent 100 years. Both economies begin

Table 4.1
Comparison of GDP per capita at different rates of growth

| Year | Growth Rate | | Difference in GDP per Capita ($) | Difference in Growth of GDP per Capita (%) |
| | 3 percent | 2 percent | | |
	GDP per Capita ($)	GDP per Capita ($)		
0	10,000	10,000	0	
1	10,300	10,200	100	1.00
2	10,609	10,404	205	2.05
5	11,593	11,041	552	5.52
10	13,439	12,190	1,249	12.49
20	18,061	14,859	3,202	32.02
30	24,273	18,114	6,159	61.59
50	43,839	26,916	16,923	169.23
100	192,186	72,446	119,740	1,197.40

with GDP per capita of $10,000. After 20 years, the economy that grew at 2 percent per year will have GDP per capita of $14,859, an increase of 149 percent. In contrast, the economy that grew at 3 percent per year will have GDP per capita of $18,061, an increase of 181 percent. The difference in total growth is therefore: 181 percent − 149 percent = 32 percent. This calculation shows that at the end of the 20-year period, the citizens in the 3 percent growth economy will be able to consume 32 percent more goods and services than the citizens in the 2 percent growth economy.

How does a 1 percent difference in annual growth lead to a difference in total growth of 32 percent over 20 years? The yearly differences in growth compound.

- At the end of the first year, the 2 percent growth economy had GDP per capita of $10,200, whereas the 3 percent growth economy had GDP per capita of $10,300, a $100 difference.
- We then apply 2 percent growth to $10,200, and 3 percent growth to $10,300.
- At the end of the second year, GDP per capita will be $10,404 in the 2 percent growth economy, and $10,609 in the 3 percent growth economy, a $205 difference.
- We then apply 2 percent growth to $10,404, and 3 percent growth to $10,609.
- Every year, the difference gets larger.
- In 30 years, the difference is $6,159. In 50 years, it is $16,923. In 100 years, it is $119,740.

Innovation and Growth

Why do some countries have higher economic growth rates than others? The work of Robert Solow, a Nobel Prize-winner in economics, has taught us a good deal about this. Solow showed that for a developed economy like the United States, technological innovation drives long-run growth rates.[3] If one developed economy had a 3 percent long-term growth rate, and another developed economy had a 2 percent long-term growth rate, it is because the economy with 3 percent growth had more innovation.

How does technological innovation contribute to growth? A simple economy can be described as having labor (people), capital (machines and other equipment), and technology. Technology reflects how well labor and capital interact to create goods and services. Technological innovation means that, for a given amount of labor and capital, an economy can create more valuable goods and services than it could before. In other words, innovation enables an economy to create more output for a given amount of resources.

In a relatively undeveloped economy, economic growth can be achieved by just adding capital, or the modern machinery used in more developed economies. If farming is done by ox and plow, and tractors are introduced, productivity will increase and faster growth will ensue. This is why China was able to grow so quickly when it began to modernize. Once an economy is full of modern technology, though, as is the case for the United States, it needs technological innovation to grow. Once every farmer has a tractor, adding more tractors won't yield more farming output. An innovation is needed, such as a new fertilizer or a new tractor that is more fuel efficient.

A single innovation can have a powerful impact on an economy because innovations can be shared and widely dispersed. If a Stone Age man found that a particular type of stone was better for making spears, other Stone Age men could copy him and begin to make spears using the same materials. In this book's Introduction, I described trade routes from 320,000 years ago in East Africa. One of the materials being transported was black obsidian, a volcanic stone that is useful for shaping into spears and other tools. The evidence suggests that different groups of humans were making spears from black obsidian; this may be the earliest example of an innovation that was shared and became widely dispersed.

Farming provides a more modern example. If a farmer finds that a fertilizer increases crop yields, other farmers can use the same type of fertilizer to increase their crop yields as well. Such farming innovations have had an immense effect on humanity. One hundred years ago, 30 percent of the U.S. population lived and worked on farms.[4] Today, only about 1 percent of the population works on farms, yet we produce more than enough food.[5] The increase in farming productivity freed up people to work on other things, like airplanes and computers, which probably would not exist if 30 percent of us were still working on farms.

The use of computers in the workplace became widespread in the 1980s, largely because of Microsoft Windows, which made computers useful for some common tasks. The fact that one business used computers to make its operations more efficient didn't prevent others from doing the same. Rather, the fact that some businesses were using computers encouraged other businesses to do the same so they could remain competitive. Today, nearly every business uses computers, and our economy is more efficient because of it.

It is common for people to argue that we are near the end of our ability to innovate. Every generation seems to think so. Paul Romer argues otherwise and uses basic physics to make his point. Everything in the universe is made of atoms. The periodic table describes the different types of atoms, or elements, of which there are about 100. Different combinations of elements produce different things. How many different things can we possibly make? Romer points out that with just four elements, there are $100 \times 99 \times 97 \times 98 = 94$ million possibilities. For things made from five elements, there are 9 billion possibilities. Using 10 elements, there are more possibilities than there are seconds since the big bang created the universe more than 13 billion years ago.[6]

Shareholder Capitalism Promotes Innovation

We know that long-term growth is important. We know that long-term growth requires innovation. Can we do anything to encourage innovation? Romer's research showed us the important role that profits play in creating an innovative economy. When a firm creates a new good or service, it holds, for some time, a monopoly on that good or service and can earn a higher rate of profit (until competitors enter the picture). If a firm discovers a new method that lowers the cost of making a product, it can earn a higher rate of profit. Profit, therefore, encourages innovation.

In a competitive economy with no innovation, *economic profits* will be zero. Economic profit is regular profit (revenues − costs), adjusted for the return you would expect to get if you instead invested in a different business of similar risk.

For example, an entrepreneur invests $1 million to start a business. The business generates $100,000 in profits each year. The return on capital is 10 percent:

$$\$100,000/\$1 \text{ million} = 10 \text{ percent}$$

If similar businesses also generate 10 percent returns, then the economic profit is zero. You could get the same return elsewhere. There is nothing special here.

A zero NPV investment is an investment for which all projected economic profits are zero. In a mature industry, it is likely that firms earn zero economic profits and that their investments are zero NPV. Zero economic profits and zero NPV investments are neither good nor bad. The value being created by this firm is the same as the value being created by other firms. The shareholders are indifferent between investing in this firm or in different firms.

Innovation can create positive NPV investments through at least two channels: (a) introducing new products and services, and (b) finding less expensive methods to make and deliver existing products and services. This situation won't be permanent, though. The high profits will attract competitors, who will either copy the innovator or introduce their own versions of the product, both of which will result in lower prices and lower profits for the innovator. Economic profits generally trend toward zero.

Innovation is costly. It is difficult to forecast which projects will result in successful innovations. Most attempts at innovation fail. Thus, profits that come from successful innovations need to be large enough to compensate for the attendant risks and costs. Governments issue patents to address this issue. Patents temporarily prevent competitors from copying an innovation. During the time that a patent is in place, the innovator holds a monopoly on that innovation and can enjoy a higher rate of profit. This encourages more investment in innovative firms and projects.

In a competitive environment, a firm has to innovate if it wants to survive. Eventually, its competitors will offer new products that displace existing ones. Competitors will find more efficient ways to manufacture and deliver products and services, lowering costs and prices. If a firm does not respond in kind, it will die. Innovation, therefore, provides both a carrot and a stick. Innovation can lead to higher profits, while not innovating may eventually drive a firm out of business.

People tend to think of companies like Tesla when they think of innovative firms. However, Ford Motor Company is also an innovative firm. Ford was founded in 1903 and more than a century later, it is still making cars. The cars that Ford makes today are nothing like the cars that it made in 1903. The manufacturing processes that Ford uses today are nothing like those it used in 1903. Ford has been continually innovating and, for this reason, it has survived.

Science and Innovation

Scientific knowledge is not the same thing as innovation. Scientific knowledge can be important and useful but, by itself, does not beget innovations that people can use in their daily lives. Business is needed for that. Profits incentivize businesses to use scientific knowledge to create innovations that benefit society. The Soviet Union had universities and government agencies that did impressive scientific research, but it had no profit-seeking firms. What products do we use that were developed by the Soviet Union? I cannot think of any. Business, therefore, is an important conduit through which science can help people.

Why don't businesses engage in basic scientific research? Because it is difficult to capture profits from a basic scientific discovery. At the same time, nonprofits and government agencies receive funding for scientific research, but they don't have a profit incentive and we rarely see innovations that are useful in everyday life coming from these institutions. Nonprofits and businesses, therefore, play different roles in creating innovation. Nonprofit institutions create general scientific knowledge, whereas firms use that knowledge to create innovations that people can use. Romer provides a nice example of this process, explaining that society's early understanding of electromagnetism "arose from research conducted in academic institutions, but magnetic tape and home videocassette recorders resulted from attempts by private firms to earn a profit."[7]

The internet is another example of how an idea that came from universities and government agencies was useless to the general public until businesses turned it into something that benefits all of society. The internet evolved from a government project known as the ARPANET (Advanced Research Projects Agency Network). The ARPANET sat idle for two decades and the public was not allowed to use it. The internet is what it is today because businesses figured out how to profit from it. The internet did not benefit society until companies like Amazon and Google found ways to make it useful to the general public. Basic research like the work that led to the ARPANET can be interesting but typically does not create things that people can use. Business is needed for that.

The mRNA COVID-19 vaccines, developed by Pfizer and Moderna, are also examples of businesses using science to make products valued by society. The science on which the vaccines are based was done by the National Institutes of Health, Dartmouth Medical School, and the Scripps Institute.[8] Pfizer and Moderna used that scientific knowledge to create a drug that people could use.

Some people complain that it is unfair that Pfizer and Moderna made such large profits from the vaccines, when some of the scientific knowledge they used came from nonprofits.[9] Yet if turning scientific knowledge into drugs was easy, then the National Institutes of Health, Dartmouth Medical School, and the Scripps Institute would have made their own vaccines. Other pharmaceutical companies would also be making their own mRNA COVID-19 vaccines. Companies attempt to use scientific knowledge to make drugs all the time, and it usually results in expensive failure. Drug development is not as simple as just reading science and then making drugs. It involves making numerous risky investments that usually fail and then hopefully having a few large successes that pay for the many failures.

Even though firms do make large profits from innovations, the full value of these innovations is not captured by the innovating firm. Instead, most of the value is enjoyed by other stakeholders and members of society. The economist William

Nordhaus, a winner of the Nobel Prize in Economics, estimates that only 2.2 percent of the social surplus from innovations is captured by firms via profits. The remaining 97.8 percent is captured by consumers and the rest of society.[10] As Nordhaus explains:

> Most of the innovations produce social value as well as private value. When copy machines replace scribes, or computers replace hand calculations, the social cost of producing a given amount of goods and services declines. It is well established that innovators do not generally capture the entire social value of inventive and innovational activity.[11]

Pfizer and Moderna have made billions of dollars from their COVID-19 vaccines, but what is the value of those vaccines to society? The vaccines protected millions of elderly and other high risk people from severe illness and death. A case can be made that the vaccines created far more value for society than was captured in the profits of those two corporations.

5

SHAREHOLDERS AND FUNDING INNOVATION

We have established a few facts about shareholder capitalism. The goal of the firm is to create value for its shareholders. A corporate manager creates value by investing in all positive NPV projects, which are investments where the value of the output is greater than the costs. Such projects use resources that have a relatively low value to create goods and services that have a relatively high value. Such investments foster economic growth and raise our standard of living. In a developed economy, positive NPV investments often result from innovation. Innovation includes creating new or improved goods and services and finding more efficient ways to make existing ones. A developed economy cannot grow without innovation. The focus of this chapter is how highly innovative investments get funded.

A firm potentially has three sources of funding for its investments. Two involve funding from shareholders.

- A firm can reinvest its accumulated profits. The firm's cash belongs to the shareholders, so internal funding comes from the shareholders.
- Issuing shares is another option. The firm can issue shares to new or existing shareholders and use the proceeds to fund its investments.

- Issuing debt is the third choice. The firm can borrow through a bank loan or bond issue.

For a variety of reasons, highly innovative firms, especially the younger ones, rely on shareholders for funding.[1]

Highly Innovative Firms Are Poorly Suited for Debt

When a firm borrows, it gets a lump sum of cash in exchange for a promise to pay back the loan at a later date, along with interest. Debt, therefore, requires the firm to make scheduled payments. But innovation is risky, and the cash flow of highly innovative firms is often unpredictable. Furthermore, many young firms, especially those focused on technology and biotechnology, generate losses instead of profits. Often these young firms are still developing their initial products and have no revenues before their products are completed. Such firms can't make debt payments.

Creditors often ask firms to pledge tangible assets as collateral. If a firm fails to make its loan payments and enters bankruptcy, the creditor has a claim to the pledged assets. Yet highly innovative firms tend to invest heavily in R&D, rather than in tangible assets, like property and heavy machinery, and thus lack collateral to pledge.

The risk and reward profile of highly innovative firms makes lending to them unattractive. Innovative investments can be characterized by a high probability of failure, along with a small chance of a large upside. Creditors get fixed payments, so they are exposed to the high risk of failure, but do not gain anything more if the firm is successful.

In contrast, none of these features are problems for shareholders. Shareholders do not require scheduled payments or collateral when investing, and they reap the gains if the firm succeeds. For these reasons, highly innovative firms tend to be financed more by shareholders than by creditors.[2]

Innovative Firms and Initial Public Offerings

If a firm needs to raise large amounts of capital from shareholders, an IPO may be its best bet. A private corporation that has not launched an IPO faces several restrictions on its ability to issue new shares. The number of shareholders is legally limited, shares cannot be sold to the general public, and shares cannot trade on a stock exchange. Companies that have gone public do not face those restrictions.

Table 5.1 summarizes all of the IPOs in the United States since 1980. Many can be described as highly innovative firms that needed external funding but were poorly suited for debt financing. Over the entire period, almost half of the IPOs were either technology or biotechnology firms, the majority of which had negative profits. During the period 2000–2021, the majority of IPOs were either technology or biotechnology firms, with

Table 5.1
Summary of IPOs: 1980–2021 and 2000–2021

Type of Company	Number of IPOs	Firms with Negative Profits (%)	Median Sales (2014$, millions)
Period: 1980–2021			
Tech	3,299	53	39.1
Biotech	1,008	88	1.6
Other	4,781	25	114
Period: 2000–2021			
Tech	846	68	113.7
Biotech	635	95	0.0
Other	1,090	37	330.6

Source: Jay R. Ritter, IPO Data, University of Florida Warrington College of Business, https://site.warrington.ufl.edu/ritter/ipo-data/.

68 percent and 95 percent, respectively, having negative profits. Since 2000, the median biotechnology IPO had no sales. Debt was not an option for many of these firms, but all of them were able to raise capital by issuing shares. The majority of these IPO firms had previously sold shares to venture capitalists when they were private corporations.

Why are shareholders willing to invest in firms that lose money and, in some cases, don't even have established products? Such firms are risky, but when they succeed, there can be an enormous upside. Moderna was among these IPOs. It went public in 2018, valued at about $7.5 billion and with a loss of $388.9 million that same year. Moderna never made a profit before its COVID-19 vaccine. Yet, investors saw that Moderna had potential and were willing to take a risk. Moderna's shareholders profited greatly when it developed its vaccine.

Some of today's most important companies, including Google, Amazon, Tesla, Apple, Dell, Microsoft, and Oracle, were also among these IPOs. There also have been many failures. It's difficult to tell in advance which companies will turn out like Google and which ones will end up like MySpace. Therefore, we need a system in which a few successes can pay for a large number of failures. Our current system does that. By the end of 2022, Tesla had earned a 13,225 percent return since its IPO in 2010.[3] That offsets a lot of failures.

Diversification and Investment in Innovation

The fact that ownership can be divided into tiny shares, as is the case with publicly traded corporations, has created an enormous amount of funding for highly innovative firms. While it is unwise to invest your entire life savings into one such firm, even highly risk-averse investors should consider investing a small part of their wealth into highly innovative firms. The reason for this is that the risk associated with most innovations is *idiosyncratic*—that is, uncorrelated with the risks that other firms face.

For example, if a firm is developing a cancer drug, the drug will either cure cancer or it will not. Interest rates, inflation, the overall stock market performance, and whether a recession is ongoing or not have no effect on the success of this drug. Finance 101 teaches us that investors can eliminate idiosyncratic risk with diversification, or by placing only a small amount of their wealth in an individual investment.

Here is an example of how diversification reduces idiosyncratic risk. Consider a company with a single project, the development of a drug that cures a type of cancer. Its possible financial returns are described in Table 5.2. The drug will be either a success or a failure. Success yields a 1,000 percent return. A $100 investment grows to $1,100. Failure means bankruptcy and the investors lose 100 percent of their investments. A $100 investment becomes $0. There is a 10 percent chance that the drug will work and a 90 percent chance that it will fail.

Most people wouldn't want to invest a large portion of their wealth in such a company. There is a 90 percent chance that they lose the entire investment. Would you want to bet your retirement on that? The *expected* return on this investment is positive though; it's 10 percent:

$$(0.9 \times -100\%) + (0.1 \times 1,000\%) = 10\%$$

If you played this game 100 times, you would expect to win 10 times and lose 90 times. The gains from the 10 wins would outweigh the 90 losses, and you would end up with a 10 percent return on your total investment.[4] The problem with investing in this one company is that the game is only played once. Even though the expected return is positive, a 90 percent chance

Table 5.2
Returns and risk of a hypothetical firm that makes a cancer-curing drug

	Success	Failure
Probability	10%	90%
Return	1,000%	–100%
$100 investment	$1,100	$0

of losing everything is too high for most people. Yet it can be beneficial to make a small investment in such a company.

To see why, let's assume that instead of just one highly innovative firm to invest in, we have many such companies. To keep things simple, let's also assume that all these companies have the same payoff structure as described in Table 5.2. Innovations tend to be unique, so we can assume that each company's product is based on a different innovation. This means that the chance of success at one company does not affect or correlate with the others. If one company fails, it tells you nothing about what will happen to the others. The returns across the companies are *uncorrelated*.[5]

Let's compare the risk of investing in different *portfolios* made up of those companies. The portfolios differ only in the number of firms that each contains. The number of firms in the portfolios ranges from 10 to 1 million. In this exercise, we assume that the *dollar amount* invested in each portfolio is the same, but the number of firms in each portfolio varies. For this reason, the portfolio weights, or the percentage of the portfolio invested in each firm, falls as the number of firms increases. For example, if the amount invested is $1 million, then $100,000 would be invested in each firm in a 10-stock portfolio, while $1,000 would be invested in each firm in a 1,000-stock portfolio. Table 5.3 shows that, as investors spread their investment across more firms,

Table 5.3

Expected returns and risk of hypothetical portfolios

Number of Firms	Portfolio Weights (1/Number of Firms) (%)	Expected Return (%)	Standard Deviation (Volatility or Risk) (%)
10	10	10	104
50	2	10	47
100	1	10	33
1,000	0.10	10	10
1,000,000	0.0001	10	0.33

the expected return of the portfolio does not change, but its risk falls.[6] Diversification can be the investor's free lunch, lowering risk, but not returns.

The expected return of a portfolio is just the average of the expected returns of the firms in the portfolio. In these portfolios, every firm has an expected return of 10 percent, so the expected return of each portfolio is 10 percent. Having more or fewer firms in the portfolio makes no difference for the portfolio's expected return.

With risk, it's a different story. A common measure of risk is the standard deviation of returns. It tells us how volatile the returns are expected to be. High volatility means that we are unsure of what we will get. A portfolio with volatile returns can have very high returns in some periods and then very low returns in others. What makes a portfolio risky is (a) the risk of the individual investments and (b) the correlation of the returns among the investments in the portfolio. We can eliminate the risk unique to each investment—the idiosyncratic risk—by making each investment a small part of the portfolio. The highly innovative firms in this example contain only idiosyncratic risk, which we can reduce or eliminate by investing a small amount in each firm.

If we assume that an investment's returns follow a normal distribution, there is a 68 percent chance that its return will be within one standard deviation of its expected return, and a 95 percent chance that its return will be within two standard deviations of its expected return. For example, a 10-stock portfolio has an expected return of 10 percent and a standard deviation of 104 percent, so there is a 95 percent chance that its return will be between 218 percent to −198 percent. We therefore have little confidence in how the 10-stock portfolio will play out. Its returns are highly volatile.

Table 5.3 shows that as the number of stocks in a portfolio increases, the standard deviation shrinks. For a 100-stock portfolio, the standard deviation is 33 percent. For a 1,000-stock portfolio, the standard deviation is 10 percent. If we have 1 million stocks, the standard deviation is only 0.33, and we are confident that the realized return will end up close to the expected return of 10% percent.

What I've described here is from Investments 101. The importance of diversification is one of the first things we teach students. Don't put all your eggs in one basket! Individual stocks are very risky. A diversified portfolio of stocks will still have risk, but less risk than an individual stock or a portfolio with a large weight placed on an individual stock.

Innovative Firms Belong in Everyone's Portfolio

Let's explore this example further to see why innovative firms belong in everyone's portfolio. A common investment portfolio is the S&P 500. It consists of 500 of the largest publicly traded corporations. Over the past 50 years, the S&P 500 had an average annual return of 9.2 percent and a standard deviation of 14.40 percent. The 100-firm innovation portfolio in Table 5.3

has slightly higher returns than the S&P 500 (10 percent versus 9.2 percent) but a much higher standard deviation (33 percent versus 14.40 percent). Yet we can use these two portfolios to make a new portfolio that has both less risk and higher returns than the S&P 500 portfolio.

The firms in the S&P 500 are more mature and less risky than the firms in the innovation portfolio. The returns of the S&P 500 stocks are influenced by the overall economy. In a recession, companies that sell pricey products and services, such as Ford and Marriott, will perform poorly, as people cut back on nonessential purchases. This performance will show up in their stock returns and in the returns of the S&P 500, which is made of these and similar firms. Therefore, the risk of the S&P 500 portfolio, which is fairly well diversified, is largely systematic risk, or risk that is common to all stocks and driven by economic conditions.

In contrast, the risk of the 100-firm innovation portfolio is entirely idiosyncratic. We can therefore assume that the 100-firm innovation portfolio's returns and the S&P 500 portfolio's expected return are uncorrelated. The S&P 500 portfolio's returns will vary over time with economic conditions, whereas the innovation portfolio's returns will not. Because the two portfolios are uncorrelated, it is possible to invest in both and get some risk reduction.

We can create a new portfolio that consists of 80 percent S&P 500 and 20 percent 100-stock innovation portfolio. The expected return of the combined 80/20 portfolio is the weighted average of the expected returns of the S&P 500 and the expected return of the 100–firm innovation portfolio. The standard deviation of the 80/20 portfolio is a function of the standard deviations of the two portfolios and their correlation, which we assumed is zero. The combined 80/20 portfolio has an expected return of 9.29 percent and a standard deviation of 13.28 percent.[7] It has both a higher expected return and less risk than the S&P 500, as shown in Table 5.4.

Table 5.4

Comparison of expected returns and risk for possible portfolios

Portfolio	Expected Return (%)	Standard Deviation (Volatility or Risk) (%)
S&P 500	9.12	14.40
100-firm innovation	10	33
Combined 80/20	9.29	13.28

Note: The combined 80/20 portfolio consists of 80% S&P 500 and 20% 100-firm innovation.

As noted earlier, what makes a portfolio risky is (a) the risk of the individual assets in the portfolio and (b) the correlation of the returns across the assets in the portfolio. You can eliminate the risk of the individual assets by making each a small part of your portfolio. In this example, each firm has only a 1 percent weight in the 100-firm innovation portfolio, which is only 20 percent of the combined 80/20 portfolio. The weights of each innovative firm in the 80/20 portfolio are tiny (1 percent × 20 percent = 0.20 percent), so each innovative firm's risk has little impact on the risk of the overall portfolio. The correlation of the innovative firms' returns with the S&P 500's returns is zero, so adding a small amount of them to a portfolio consisting of the S&P 500 adds almost no risk.[8]

It therefore can make sense to invest in virtually all publicly traded companies, including the small innovative ones specializing in risky ventures in technology and biotechnology. This can be accomplished by investing in index funds or mutual funds that include smaller companies.

How a company's ownership is structured can therefore affect what it can invest in. Diverse ownership, typical in publicly traded companies, facilitates funding for high-risk yet potentially impactful projects. Small investments from many different investors can be pooled to create a large amount of capital for highly innovative firms. Solving many of society's most vexing problems will likely require diverse ownership to manage the risks involved. While selling shares in a business will not cure cancer, funding potential cures will likely require a large number of shareholders making small investments.

For risky companies to attract investment, shareholders need to keep the gains when projects are successful. Proponents of the various social responsibility frameworks are fine with shareholders absorbing the losses, but then want to socialize the gains. But the possibility of keeping the gains is what motivates people to invest and become shareholders in the first place.

The Importance of Liquidity

Do shareholders of mature companies promote growth and innovation? Consider an investor who buys some shares of Apple, a mature, publicly traded company. As of this writing, Apple's stock price is $172.88, which means that the last trade of Apple's stock was at that price. The seller got $172.88 per share, and the buyer got the shares. Did the buyer enable anything?

Apple did not issue new stock. The seller—whether an institution or an individual investor, not Apple—got the $172.88 per share. Apple ended 2022 with about $48 billion in cash and a good deal of cash flow. It does not need to raise capital to grow. Does buying Apple's shares enable anything?

In this case, the buyer is contributing to the Apple's *liquidity*. For the seller to convert her shares to cash, she needs a buyer. At one time, the seller was a buyer. She was willing to buy Apple because its shares are *liquid*; she knew that she could sell the shares when she wanted to.

When Apple issued its IPO in 1980, its earnings were only $11.7 million. Yet its market capitalization at the end of its first day as a publicly traded company was $1.8 billion. Why were investors willing to pay so much for a young, risky company barely making a profit? One reason was the potential for future profits. Another reason was liquidity. Apple's early investors knew they could easily sell their shares when they wanted to.

Apple became a huge success, but if its investors could not sell their shares, then they could not enjoy their gains. The investors could continue to hold Apple's shares and collect dividends, but they would not have the freedom to convert their shares to cash at a time of their choosing. Illiquid assets that can't be easily converted to cash are priced at a discount relative to liquid assets. If Apple's early investors had not expected its shares to be liquid, many would not have invested, and Apple would not have been able to fund its growth and become the company it is today.

To summarize, shareholders who buy shares directly from a company enable the company to grow. The subsequent shareholders, who buy their shares on a stock exchange, create liquidity. Liquidity contributes to a company's growth because the original shareholders would have been less willing to invest if there were no liquid market in which to sell their shares. The initial investment enables growth, but the expectation of liquidity motivates the initial investment.

6

CREATIVE DESTRUCTION

The opening up of new markets, foreign or domestic, and the organizational development from the craft shop to such concerns as U.S. Steel illustrate the same process of industrial mutation—if I may use that biological term—that incessantly revolutionizes the economic structure from within, incessantly destroying the old one, incessantly creating a new one. This process of Creative Destruction is the essential fact about capitalism.[1]

—*Joseph Schumpeter*

Each year, *Fortune* magazine compiles a list of the 500 largest U.S. corporations based on revenue. Of the 500 corporations that made the list in 1955, only 52, or about 10 percent, are still among the Fortune 500 today.[2] Put differently, 90 percent of the largest companies 68 years ago have been displaced by newer companies. Such displacement is common in growing economies. Research shows that economic growth is faster in countries with greater turnover among large businesses, and slower in countries where the largest companies remain on top.[3]

Why is big business turnover associated with faster economic growth? As discussed in Chapter 4, economic growth requires innovation and innovation results in something new replacing something established. The most important innovations have tended to come from new companies. Successful innovations allow these new companies to grow and eventually replace existing firms. Companies such as Microsoft, Google, and Netflix did not exist in 1995, but are in the Fortune 500 today. Economies that produce fewer innovative firms have slower growth.

This effect was foreseen more than a century ago by the economist Joseph Schumpeter, who coined the term "creative destruction" to describe how, in a capitalist economy, new firms replace existing firms, and new business processes replace existing ones. In a growing economy, there is always creation and creation results in destruction. Schumpeter told us that creative destruction is the "essential fact" about capitalism—its central driving force—and he was right.

Capitalism, therefore, does not favor big business. Capitalism can be described as *pro-business*, but it does not favor any particular type of business. Capitalism does not favor Amazon over an upstart trying to upend Amazon. In a capitalist economy, firms are always being born and firms are always dying, or the economy will not grow.

Creative destruction means that some people suffer in the short term even as society's overall wealth grows. When a business is on the destruction side and begins to shrink or fail, its stakeholders suffer. Its employees lose jobs, its suppliers lose a customer, its creditors may not get paid back, and its shareholders are made poorer. By the same token, when a business is on the creation side of things, its stakeholders benefit.

It is important to recognize that letting unprofitable firms die is as important as enabling profitable firms to grow. An unprofitable firm uses society's scarce resources in a manner that does not benefit society. It uses society's resources to create something of lesser value than the resources used. It's better if the assets and employees of unprofitable firms are redeployed elsewhere in the economy where they can create value.

Freedom of Choice and Creative Destruction

Ultimately, it is the stakeholders who decide which firms succeed and which firms fail. To survive, a firm needs to earn a profit. A profit is a leftover that the firm's owners get to keep after having made all the firm's other stakeholders—such as customers, employees, suppliers, and creditors—better off. If a firm cannot contract with its stakeholders in such a way that it can earn a profit, then it will fail. We could also say that society decides which firms survive and which ones fail. If a firm can't use resources on which society places a lower value to create goods and services on which society places a higher value, then the firm will fail.

For example, Amazon is successful because its customers like the service it provides, its suppliers are willing to sell their products on its platform, and its employees are willing to work for it. It operates within the rules and regulations set by various governments. Someday, one or all these things will change, and Amazon will die. Its shareholders do not get to decide if or when that will happen.

Consumers are major catalysts of creative destruction. We want the best new products, and we want each product at the lowest price. Most of us are not very loyal to a specific brand or company. If a better mousetrap comes along, or if the same mousetrap can be had for a lower price, we tend to switch products. When consumers switch, jobs may be destroyed at the losing firm.

Unfortunately, we can't have it both ways. If we want choice as consumers, then we must accept instability in employment. For that matter, if we want economic growth, then we must tolerate instability in employment. Growth requires innovation, and innovation means some businesses get destroyed when new ones are created.

When employees lose their jobs, they and their families face hardships. No one likes to see this. But what is the alternative? Do we force firms to pay people for work that no longer creates something of greater value? In 1900, 109,000 people in the United States were employed as carriage and harness makers.[4] The railroad and automobile destroyed those jobs. Would it be better if we still paid people to make carriages and harnesses that are never used? In 1920, 2.1 million Americans, about 2 percent of the population, worked for railroads. Today, only 200,000 Americans work for railroads, or 0.06 percent of the population.[5] Railroads became more efficient, carrying more freight today than in 1920, and the automobile displaced many needs for railroads. Would we be better off if we paid 2 percent of the population to do railroad work that is no longer needed? We can't blame firms when jobs are destroyed; they are only responding to what consumers want. If people no longer want to buy horse-drawn carriages, we cannot blame firms for not making them.

When a firm and an employee agree to an employment contract, both sides benefit. The employee is trading with the firm's owners, the shareholders. The employee gets wages and the shareholders get the value created by the employee's labor. If over time, one side no longer sees a benefit from the arrangement, then that party should be allowed to exit. If an employee no longer finds it to her benefit to work at the firm, she ought to leave. Likewise, if an employee's labor no longer creates value for the firm, then the firm should end the employment, as the wage is no longer part of a mutually beneficial trade. If firms are unable to discharge employees in such cases, then firms will be reluctant to hire people, and we will have fewer jobs and a less robust economy.

We must keep in mind that destruction is only half the picture and not overlook the creation side of things. Most jobs today did not exist in 1920. The largest private employer in the United

States is currently Walmart, founded in 1962. The second largest is Amazon, founded in 1994. Walmart and Amazon destroyed many jobs as they grew into the firms they are today, but at the same time, both created many jobs. There were no computers in 1920, so many computer-related jobs—such as computer manufacturing, chip manufacturing, and software development—came into being only during the past half century. More generally, 10 percent of U.S. jobs did not exist one year ago, and 10 percent of jobs will not exist one year from now.[6] A century from now, today's jobs either will be done much differently, with the aid of new technologies, or will no longer exist. There will be jobs in industries that have not been invented yet, just as today's job in software development, air travel, and biotechnology did not exist 100 years ago.

Creative destruction leads to economic growth and growth means that our children and grandchildren will live better than we do. Global GDP per capita is currently $12,235.[7] If the global economy grows at an average of 2 percent per year over the next century, global GDP per capita will reach $88,638, a 724 percent increase. The wealth of people then will be much greater than ours now. They will have technologies that we have not dreamed of. For that to happen, almost all the businesses and business processes we see today must be replaced with something new and better. Creation and destruction are intrinsically linked. If we want the benefits of creation, we have to live with the destruction.

Capitalism and Sustainability

In the third section of the book, I will discuss "sustainability," the ubiquitous term that has become a mantra at business schools and in the corporate world. There is much discussion about what constitutes a "sustainable business" and a "sustainable business practice." Yet we have not had sustainable businesses or business

practices since the beginning of the modern industrial era. Nor
will there be, as long as the economy continues to grow.

Before the Industrial Revolution, which began around the
year 1800, there was no persistent economic growth. There was
little in the way of innovation, and things would continue in the
same way for centuries. Living standards did not improve. Businesses and business practices at that time could be described as
sustainable. For example, the first evidence of blacksmithing is
from 1350 BCE in Egypt.[8] Two thousand years later in medieval
Europe, you could have the same job.

But such stasis is not the case in a modern capitalist economy
that is characterized by creative destruction and the sustained
economic growth it makes possible. Recall that 90 percent of the
Fortune 500 companies in 1955 are not among the Fortune 500
today. We should expect the same to happen going forward, as
long as there is economic growth. If an economy is growing, then
no business or business process is sustainable. All will eventually
be destroyed. Which firms will be destroyed and when is unpredictable because innovation is, by definition, unpredictable.

Capitalism, therefore, creates two seemingly conflicting processes that are really two sides of the same coin. We can have
sustainable economic growth, but if we do, then nothing is sustainable
at the level of the individual business. In order for the economy
to grow, processes within businesses must be replaced and new
businesses must displace old ones. Creative destruction is effectively the absence of sustainability at the individual business level.
If there is no creative destruction, it means there is no meaningful
innovation, and without innovation there is no sustained economic growth. Therefore, it does not make sense to call a business
"sustainable" in a modern economy characterized by creative
destruction and growth.

7

LESSONS FROM COMMUNISM

The preceding chapters explained what shareholder capitalism is and why it benefits everyone in society, not just shareholders. To summarize, the goal of the corporate manager is to maximize shareholder value, which is driven by the expected profits over the life of the firm. Profits are a leftover that the shareholders get to keep, after the firm's other stakeholders have been made better off. Profits reflect the difference in value between what a firm makes and the resources it uses. Profits therefore direct society's scarce resources to their best use.

Furthermore, profits incentivize innovation, which is necessary for the prolonged economic growth that improves our standard of living. Shareholders are willing to finance innovation and potentially profitable firms and thus move their capital to its best use, which enables economic growth.

If we want to better understand the effectiveness of capitalism, it can be useful to examine what happens in its absence. What happens if there are no profit-seeking firms? Enterprises don't base decisions on what to make by calculating expected profits. Instead, government planners tell each enterprise what to produce, how to produce it, and in what quantity. Enterprises and their various stakeholders, such as customers, suppliers, and employees, don't choose to transact with one another but instead are assigned to each other by the government. Prices are set by the government, not by supply and demand. How does this all work out?

We know the answer because such an experiment was run during the 20th century. During much of that time, it was common for intellectuals to claim that capitalism was unsustainable and that socialism was the answer. I use the words "communism" and "socialism" interchangeably, as did Karl Marx and Friedrich Engels. As capitalism largely depends on individuals making decisions freely in the marketplace, the alleged solutions to capitalism's problems always entail restricting individual choice in some way. Communism is an extreme example of this.

I am not equating communism with the various corporate social responsibility frameworks that I critique in the third section of the book. My goal in this first section of the book is to explain what makes capitalism such an effective economic system. I tried to show that having firms pursue profits benefits both shareholders *and other stakeholders.* Society as a whole is better off. Examining the history and performance of a system that prohibited private enterprise can help us appreciate capitalism's effects. If we get rid of profit maximization as businesses' top priority, are consumers better off? Are workers better off? Are customer-supplier relations better? Do resources get used more efficiently? Are people's lives better?

To study these questions, this chapter presents three historical case studies. The first is a cross-country comparison. It compares the economic performance of the Soviet Union with that of the United States and other developed Western economies during the Cold War. The second examines how the economic performance of a single country, China, changed over time when it moved from strict communism to a more market-based system after reforms during the leadership of Deng Xiaoping. The third examines Germany, which was split into two countries, one communist and one capitalist, and then reunited.

The Soviet Union

The Communists took control of Russia in 1917. In 1922, the Soviet Union was established. It collapsed in 1991. In 1989, two of its senior economists, Nikolai Shmelev and Vladimir Popov, published a book, *The Turning Point*, that explains how the Soviet economy operated and assessed its performance.[1] The book was written during the period known as Perestroika, when the government of Mikhail Gorbachev allowed for greater public discussion of topics previously deemed controversial. It is doubtful that such a candid description of the Soviet economy would have been made public before that period. The book's central conclusion is that, relative to capitalism, a planned economy will always be plagued by inefficiency. There are always persistent surpluses of some things and persistent shortages of others. Without market prices and the incentives created by the profit motive, resources are not allocated efficiently. The book is full of tragic and yet instructive examples.

The Soviet economy was plagued by waste. In a capitalist economy, where firms are motivated by profits, there is an incentive to use resources efficiently. Waste results in higher costs and lower profits. Capitalists seek profits for their own self-interest, but the end result is that they use society's scarce resources carefully. In the Soviet economy, there were no such incentives, and waste was rampant. A chapter titled "Black Holes That Swallow Resources" describes this effect:

> The pervasive waste and profligate use of resources is striking. We produce and purchase machines that no one needs, which gather dust in warehouses or rust outdoors. We build enterprises in places where there are no workers available because

of "labor shortages." At the same time there is a drastic short-
age of equipment and insufficient production capacity. . . . It
takes eleven to twelve years to carry out a construction project,
in contrast to one and a half to two years everywhere else in
the world.[2]

OK, so maybe there was too much waste. But weren't people
more cooperative? The entire point of communism is to make a
more communal society. How did that go? In the Soviet Union,
"trading partners" were assigned. Instead of firms choosing their
suppliers, government planners assigned these relations. Here is
how that went:

> If a top business executive reports to a planner that his trading
> partners [enterprises assigned by planners to provide goods and
> service to one another] failed him and delivered nuts instead of
> bolts or the other way around, their trading partner, in turn,
> will blame suppliers, and so on, so that it is impossible to find
> the guilty party. This annoys the planner, since it looks as if the
> executive is hinting that something wasn't anticipated "from
> above." And consequently he, the planner, is to blame. Having
> learned from experience, the planner simply refuses to accept
> such arguments. "If you couldn't get it," he tells the executive,
> "it means you should have made it yourself." And that's what
> they end up doing.[3]

In contrast, profit seeking encourages firms to treat their customers well. If a supplier is unreliable with either product quality
or timeliness, its customers can find a different supplier. That
gives profit-seeking firms an incentive to keep their customers
happy. The Soviets removed competition and profits from this
equation, and it didn't work. Why should it? Profits create a carrot and a stick. If you make your customers happy, your wealth
increases. If you treat your customers badly, they leave, and you
go out of business. The Soviet system took away both the carrot
and the stick.

What was it like to be a consumer in the Soviet Union? In our economy, retail stores have to compete with one another for customers. If a store doesn't offer the products that people want at a price that they are willing to pay, they don't have to shop there. Retail stores therefore have an incentive to make consumers happy. Those that don't go out of business.

It is different in a planned economy. There are stores that exist and that is all. It's like the Department of Motor Vehicles for all things retail. You can go there and wait for your license, or you don't get a license. There is no other choice. On top of that, the Soviet economy had an entire supply chain full of enterprises with little incentive to make their trading partners happy. In a world without competition and profits, what does it matter if the products are of low quality, arrive late, or not at all? It is not surprising that here in the United States, the word "Soviet" was for some time slang for low quality and poor service.

This passage from a 1982 *New York Times* article titled "Soviet Food Shortages: Grumbling and Excuses" describes what it was like to shop for groceries in the Soviet Union:

> At noontime one day last week the meat counter was down to pitiful cuts of beef and mutton, mostly fat and bone. After a few weeks late last year when it disappeared from Moscow shops, butter was on sale again, but with a limit of 1.1 pounds per shopper. The vegetable counter boasted symmetrically arranged displays of carrots, beetroot and cabbage, but much of it was rotten. . . . A foreigner not long in the Soviet Union who visited the shop whispered his surprise to a Muscovite companion. But the man was not dismayed. "Comparatively speaking, this is really quite good, better than many of the stores in the suburbs," he said. "There, you're lucky to find butter at all, and there's hardly ever any mutton."[4]

The *Times* article goes on to explain how government officials blamed the weather. Here in the United States, we also have adverse weather events, but we do not face food shortages. The Soviet Union had trouble feeding itself because it eliminated mutually beneficial trading. It eliminated profit making. It eliminated competition. When you take all of that away, people have little incentive to produce goods and services. As Adam Smith taught us more than 200 years ago:

> It is not from the benevolence of the butcher, the brewer, or the baker that we expect our dinner, but from their regard to their own self-interest. We address ourselves not to their humanity but to their self-love, and never talk to them of our own necessities, but of their advantages.[5]

Today, we can walk into a grocery store in the United States and find shelves stocked with goods from all over the world. In contrast to not being able to find butter, as was the case in the Soviet Union, we have a difficult decision to make over which butter to buy. Grass-fed? Organic? My local grocer offers butter from France, Finland, Ireland, and the United States.

Why do we find ourselves with such an abundance of butter? Because it is profitable to make and sell butter. Farmers, butter makers, distributors, and stores all find it profitable to participate in the production, distribution, and sale of butter. Each entity in the butter supply chain engages in mutually beneficial trading. No government agency is in charge of making sure that we have enough butter. We have enough butter because the marketplace rewards the people who supply it.

What is true for butter is true for any good or service. Why do we have an abundance of bread, meat, ice cream, flat-screen TVs, automobiles, and smartphones? Because firms find it profitable to create and distribute them. No single person or entity is tasked with creating any of these products. Mutually beneficial trading is what causes them to be produced.

The Turning Point also compares the macroeconomic performance of the Soviet economy with that of capitalist economies. All economies have scarce resources that have alternative uses. The system that takes those scarce resources and creates the maximum amount of goods and services delivers the highest standard of living to its citizens. By this metric, the Soviet economy performed terribly. In a section titled "Material Shortages and Surplus Inventories," the Soviet economists give salient examples of how inefficient their economy was:

- The Soviet Union used 1.5 times more materials, 2.1 times more energy, and 2.4 times more metal to create a unit of national income than the United States did.
- Soviet agricultural production was 15 percent less than that of the United States but used 3.5 times more energy.
- To make one ton of copper, the Soviets used 1,000 kilowatt-hours compared with 300 hours for West Germany.
- To produce one ton of cement, the Soviets used twice as much energy as Japan.

The Turning Point was published with the hope that the Soviet economy could be reformed and that the Soviet Union would live on. Instead, the Soviet Union collapsed just a couple of years later.

Mao's China versus the Growth That Followed

In 1949, Chinese Communist Party forces captured the Chinese capital Beijing (then Peking), and communist leader Mao Zedong proclaimed the founding of the People's Republic of China. There were two largely opposing sets of policies in China during the second half of the 20th century. One set of policies went all in on communism. It did everything it could to get rid of private property and profit incentives. A subsequent set of policies did the opposite, going so far as to celebrate profit making and entrepreneurship. How did the Chinese people fare under each?

The first set of policies was part of the Great Leap Forward, the name for China's five-year plan for the period 1958–1962. Mao decided that China needed to industrialize and to do so quickly. The goal was to catch up to Great Britain in 15 years. China was a poor country then, with much of its population living in small villages and working on family farms. The Great Leap Forward aimed to reorganize the peasant population to industrialize China while simultaneously improving its agricultural output.

Everything in the countryside was forcibly collectivized. Peasant households were organized into cooperatives. By the end of 1958, the entire Chinese countryside had been organized into communes. Private property, including land, tools, and livestock, was confiscated. There were communal kitchens and cooking at home was banned. Food was distributed based on merit, which was determined by those who distributed the food. Those who did not support the party's edict did not eat.

In *Mao's Great Famine*, historian Frank Dikötter uses archival records from China to paint a picture of what happened during this time. He estimates that there were 45 million premature deaths over this five-year period. Of these, 6 million to 8 million people were "buried alive, tortured or beaten to death." Of those who starved, many died not because there was no food, but because "they were deliberately and selectively deprived of food by local cadres because they were relatively rich, dragged their feet, spoke out, or simply were not liked, for whatever reason, by whoever wielded the canteen ladle."[6] I'll spare you the details from Dikötter's chapter on cannibalism.

Mao died in 1976, and Deng Xiaoping took over in 1978. Deng introduced a series of reforms that took China away from a

Marxist economy and toward a more capitalist one with privately owned farms and profit-seeking firms. Foreign investment was welcome. Free trade expanded within China and between China and other nations.

During Mao's tenure, persons who tried to make extra money for themselves were persecuted and brutally punished. Under Deng's reign, such entrepreneurial activity was celebrated. Beginning in 1979, the government began to promote entrepreneurship, and new phrases were introduced into the language to promote profit seeking among small farmers. Daniel Keliher writes about the new phrases in *Peasant Power in China*:

> The first new term, "zhuanye hu" (specialized household), saturated rural news reporting. These entrepreneurial households became ubiquitous media heroes, celebrated in newspapers and romanticized in the movies. "Wan yuan hu," or 10,000-yuan households, were another new category, made of families whose annual income reached the fabulous level of ten thousand yuan—roughly ten times the income of most peasant households. Another neologism was "jingji liangheti" . . . referred to business on a larger scale that pooled capital from several or many households and paid out dividends and profits according to investment share.[7]

Another important factor in China's economic reforms was its establishment of special economic zones. The first four were established in 1979 in Shenzhen, Shantou, Xiamen, and Zhuhai.[8] These zones were allowed to pursue more market-oriented economic policies than the rest of China. Although they were a limited and selective form of economic liberalization, the zones worked so well that in 1986 China added 14 more zones.[9] It has since added additional free trade zones, economic and technological zones, and high-tech industrial and development zones. The success of these zones suggests that it would be beneficial to extend such market-friendly policies to the entire country, but the

Chinese government has not shown any indication that it plans to do so.

The economist Paul Romer writes that if Shenzhen were a city-state like Singapore, it would have set the record for the fastest economic growth of any country.[10] Shenzhen grew, in per capita terms, at 23 percent per year during 1980–1985, and then at 7 percent per year during 1985–2011. A 7 percent annual growth rate means doubling the standard of living every 10 years. During this time, Shenzhen's population increased from 300,000 to more than 10 million.

How did these reforms affect the poorest people in China? Forty years later, China's economic reforms have made it possible for nearly 800 million people to rise out of poverty.[11] It is the largest poverty reduction in human history. Compare that to the death and destruction caused by the Great Leap Forward.

The German Experiment

The splitting of Germany after World War II provides an unfortunate natural experiment to compare how people fare under capitalism and communism. The Soviet Union created a communist country in the East, while the United States and its allies established a capitalist one in the West. How did the citizens of each country fare? In the West, wealth and freedom reigned. In the East, poverty and totalitarianism reigned, as is always the case with communism.

When Germany was divided in 1949, each of the two countries had a GDP per capita that was about equal. At the time of reunification in 1990, West Germany's GDP per capita was more than twice that of East Germany's.[12] At its founding, East Germany had a population of 18.4 million, which had shrunk to 16.4 million by 1990, when it was absorbed into West Germany.[13] During that time, 2.7 million people, 16 percent of the initial population, fled

East Germany to the West.[14] It has been 32 years since the German reunification. Since then, the former East Germany has received $2 trillion in subsidies from what was West Germany, yet eastern Germany still lags behind the country's west economically.[15]

For most of East Germany's existence, its citizens were not allowed to emigrate. Trying to do so was risky; people were often shot while attempting to escape.[16] German historians estimate that 75,000 persons were jailed for trying to escape, with a punishment of one to two years in prison.[17] Among these were 5,500 East German border guards. Another 2,500 border guards did manage to escape.[18]

A major reason that East Germans wanted to leave was that, compared with Germans in the West, they lived under tyranny and were poor as a result. A 1990 *New York Times* article titled "East Germany's Economy Far Sicker Than Expected" was published a few weeks before the reunification.[19] At that time, Western companies were visiting East Germany, looking for enterprises to buy and invest in. What they found surprised them. The executives were "shocked by the sorry state of most East German factories and the scarcity of business skills."[20]

The East German government offered to return a factory that had belonged to an Italian company, the Olivetti Group, before World War II. Although the factory was offered for free, the Olivetti Group turned it down because the restructuring costs would have been too high. The building and machinery were in poor condition and outdated, and the workforce was too inefficient. The East German government also proposed a joint venture with the Olivetti Group that would have employed 12,000 East German workers. Olivetti also turned down that offer, because it concluded that it could get the same production from 900 workers in West Germany.[21]

A West German taxi company tried to set up a joint venture in the city of Leipzig in East Germany. It was willing to provide new Mercedes-Benz taxis and a modern radio dispatch system. The deal never happened. One of the West German taxi entrepreneurs remarked that the East Germans they dealt with "were friendly and nice, but they weren't creative thinkers in an economic sense. . . . New ideas struck them as totally strange."[22]

The first West German company to attempt a joint venture with an East German partner tried to build a factory to produce compact discs. East Germany's communist bureaucracy slowed the process so much that the factory was never built. A company spokesman said, "It all dragged out forever; if we had our way, we would have started building there months ago. . . . And in the meantime, the East German economy died."[23]

When given the choice, East German consumers avoided products made by East German enterprises.[24] They considered East German products to be of low quality and preferred products from Western companies. That ultimately led to the failure of most East German enterprises.

Communism's Legacy of Poverty and Tyranny

All three of the cases presented here show that communism leads to terrible economic performance. Why is this so? In communism, there are no market prices and no profit incentives. In a market economy, prices reflect supply and demand. Scarcer resources, which have a high demand relative to supply, command higher prices. In a communist economy, central planners invent the prices. Without market prices, there is no way to tell the value that society places on something. Market prices reflect society's wants and needs; invented prices do not. Are we using our scarce resources to create products that are more valuable than the resource being used? There is no way to tell without market prices that function freely.

In a world without profits, there is no incentive to create the goods and services that society wants and needs. Why should a communist enterprise manager care if its customers, or any other stakeholders, are happy? Under capitalism, if a firm cannot create value for its stakeholders, they do not trade with it, and it goes out of business. Under communism, trading partners are assigned, and stakeholders are stuck with each other. There is no incentive to use resources more efficiently. Why should a manager care if costs are lower when there are no profits? There is no incentive to innovate, as it won't make the innovator any richer.

Critics of shareholder capitalism claim that if businesses were to focus on metrics besides profits, everyone would act nicer, and the world would be a better place. This claim overlooks the fact that the largest atrocities of the 20th century resulted from an ideology that is largely based on getting rid of the profit motive. *The Black Book of Communism* estimates that, during the 20th century, communist governments killed 94 million of their own people.[25] The book *Death by Government* estimates 110 million deaths.[26] As in China, the deaths in other communist countries resulted from economic policies that created famines and political purges.

As I mention at the beginning of this chapter, I am not arguing that the various corporate social responsibility frameworks will lead to Soviet-style communism. However, the results from communism do show that taking away the profit motive as the principal basis for business decision making leads to a worse allocation of resources and makes everyone poorer in the long run. The more the profit motive is eroded, the worse such impoverishment will be. Therefore, we should avoid policies that erode the profit motive as the corporate managers' top priority.

Part Two

COMMON FALLACIES

8

THE STAKEHOLDER FALLACY

The key insight of Adam Smith's *Wealth of Nations* is misleadingly simple: if an exchange between two parties is voluntary, it will not take place unless both believe they will benefit from it. Most economic fallacies derive from the neglect of this simple insight, from the tendency to assume that there is a fixed pie, that only one party can gain at the expense of the other.[1]

—*Milton Friedman and Rose Friedman*

More than 200 years after Adam Smith wrote *The Wealth of Nations*, many people still do not understand that voluntary trade benefits both parties. This has led to the popular misperception that because shareholder capitalism puts the interests of shareholders first, it overlooks the firm's other stakeholders. I refer to this common misunderstanding as the "stakeholder fallacy."

Proponents of the stakeholder fallacy argue that a "fairer" form of capitalism would put shareholders and other stakeholders on equal footing. This overlooks the fact that they already are on equal footing. If a customer or an employee in a capitalist economy doesn't find it beneficial to transact with a firm, then she isn't required to do so. By the same token, if a transaction doesn't benefit the firm's shareholders, then the firm shouldn't engage in the transaction. That is all shareholder capitalism requires.

More generally, in capitalism transactions happen only if both sides expect to benefit. If two Stone Age men agree to trade spears for furs, both are made better off by the trade. If Apple sells me an iPhone, Apple's shareholders and I are both made better off by the trade. My buying the iPhone from Apple is just a modern form of trading. The principle of mutual benefit, though, is the same as it has been for thousands of years. When people trade with a corporation like Apple, they are ultimately trading with the people who own the business—the shareholders.

The stakeholder fallacy stems partly from misunderstanding, but other agendas are likely at play. This fallacy is promoted by people who would like to use business to promote their own ideological agendas. It's easier to direct resources away from normal business activities when you have convinced others that normal business is bad for society.

Klaus Schwab and the World Economic Forum

Klaus Schwab and the World Economic Forum (WEF), which Schwab founded and leads, are prominent and longtime critics of shareholder capitalism. The WEF is an international nonprofit organization that Schwab established in 1971 in Cologny, Switzerland. To say that it is influential would be an understatement. The WEF is perhaps best known for its annual meeting in Davos, Switzerland. The 2022 meeting had 2,500 leaders from politics, business, civil society, and media in attendance.[2] The attendees included 50 heads of government—including Chinese President Xi Jinping and German Chancellor Olaf Scholz—and 1,250 leaders from the private sector.[3] The U.S. delegation included multiple senators and members of Congress and two representatives from the White House. There were 400 persons in attendance from the press.[4]

The WEF is primarily funded by fees it charges corporations for various types of partnerships and membership.[5] Its 850 partners include some of the most important multinational corporations, such as Apple, Amazon, Google, Microsoft, Boeing, BlackRock, JPMorgan Chase, Bank of America, Huawei, and Bank of China.[6]

Schwab is a former business management professor. Throughout its history, the WEF has engaged with academic institutions, which may help explain why some of the fallacies it promotes are popular at business schools.[7] The WEF's first annual meeting in 1971 included 50 academics described as "prominent professors from the top US business schools."[8] Its Global University Leaders Forum, initiated in 2009, "integrated the presidents of the world's 25 top academic institutions into the Forum's networks and activities."[9] Member universities include Harvard, Stanford, Princeton, and Oxford.

The WEF, under Schwab's direction, has worked tirelessly for years to promote the stakeholder fallacy. You can find examples of it on the WEF website, in WEF marketing materials, and in Schwab's writings. One could even say that the WEF's founding was based on the stakeholder fallacy. The WEF's institutional brochure describes how a book by Schwab on this topic inspired the first Davos meeting in 1971 and led to the creation of the WEF:

> I wrote a book on modern management describing what is today called the stakeholder concept. It recognized that the business of business was not simply serving shareholder interests, but everyone who has a stake in the "well-being" of the enterprise: employees, customers and society.[10]

What Schwab overlooks is that "serving shareholder interests" raises the well-being of the other stakeholders. Employees and customers have their interests served by the business, or the business has no customers, no employees, no profits, and no ability to keep operating. To create wealth for its shareholders, a business *must consider* the well-being of its other stakeholders.

In 2020, the WEF celebrated its 50th anniversary. To mark this milestone, the WEF published the "Davos Manifesto 2020," which it describes as "a set of ethical principles to guide companies in the age of the Fourth Industrial Revolution." (So much for modest goals.) The manifesto begins by stating the following:

> The purpose of a company is to engage all its stakeholders in shared and sustained value creation. In creating such value, a company serves not only its shareholders, but all its stakeholders—employees, customers, suppliers, local communities and society at large.[11]

A company cannot serve "only its shareholders." That is impossible. Shareholders are served by consistent profits. To earn consistent profits, a firm must consistently serve its other stakeholders. It must make products that its customers value. It must offer wages and work conditions that attract employees. It must buy products from suppliers at prices that create profits for the suppliers. It must pay taxes. It must comply with the rules and regulations that are placed on it by the government it operates under. All these things must be accomplished for a firm to make a profit and create wealth for its shareholders. This is as much a fact of life as plants needing water and sunshine to grow. If you want your plants to grow, water them and let them get sunlight. If you want your business to grow, you need to enter mutually beneficial agreements with your stakeholders, who are free to choose whether to transact with your business or not.

The Business Roundtable CEOs

The Business Roundtable is an association of CEOs from some of America's largest corporations. As of 2019, these CEOs led companies that employed 20 million people and generated $7 trillion in revenues.[12] Building on Schwab's insights, the Business Roundtable in 2019 updated its Statement on the Purpose of a Corporation. The updated Statement is based on the stakeholder fallacy. As the accompanying 2019 press release said, it was "signed by 181 CEOs who commit to lead their companies for the benefit of all stakeholders—customers, employees, suppliers, communities and shareholders."[13] The updated Statement states:

> Since 1978, Business Roundtable has periodically issued Principles of Corporate Governance that include language on the purpose of a corporation. Each version of that document issued since 1997 has stated that corporations exist principally to serve their shareholders. It has become clear that this language on corporate purpose does not accurately describe the ways in which we and our fellow CEOs endeavor every day to create value for all our stakeholders, whose long-term interests are inseparable.[14]

Do the Business Roundtable CEOs really believe that a business can serve its shareholders without benefiting the other stakeholders? Here are some questions I would like to ask the CEOs who signed the 2019 statement:

1. How did the Business Roundtable member companies get to the point of collectively having $7 trillion in revenues if they were not making their customers better off?
2. Why do 20 million people choose to work at Business Roundtable companies if they do not make their employees better off?
3. Have Business Roundtable companies been beneficial to the local communities in which they operate? Would these communities be better off if the firms left? Have local governments tried to get them to leave?

What the 2019 Business Roundtable Statement does is give CEOs a license to use their firms' resources to pursue their own agendas. You can justify almost any business decision by claiming that some stakeholder somewhere is made better off because of it. The CEO can then be a philosopher-king, rather than an employee who works for the company's shareholders.

Larry Fink and BlackRock

Larry Fink is the CEO of BlackRock, the world's largest institutional investor. BlackRock had more than $9 trillion in assets under management at the end of the first quarter of 2023.[15] When a BlackRock fund buys a share of stock, BlackRock is technically the shareholder, and it gets to vote on various corporate decisions. If you invest in a BlackRock fund and it buys ExxonMobil, the fund is the shareholder of ExxonMobil, not you. BlackRock and Fink thus wield considerable influence over the corporations in which BlackRock invests. In the third section of this book, I will discuss how they have used that influence to engage in political activism.

Fink writes an annual letter to the CEOs of the companies that BlackRock invests in, often telling them how they should be running their businesses. In his 2022 letter, Fink lectured on the need to develop "mutually beneficial relationships" with stakeholders:

> Stakeholder capitalism is not about politics. . . . It is capitalism, driven by mutually beneficial relationships between you and the employees, customers, suppliers, and communities your company relies on to prosper. . . . In today's globally interconnected world, a company must create value for and be valued by its full range of stakeholders in order to deliver long-term value for its shareholders. It is through effective stakeholder capitalism that capital is efficiently allocated, companies achieve durable profitability, and value is created and sustained over the long-term.[16]

We could replace the word "stakeholder capitalism" with "shareholder capitalism" and write the same thing. It has always been the case that the firm, if it is to create value for shareholders, it must also create value for its stakeholders. Such has been true for all businesses for as long as there have been businesses.

Here are some questions that I would like to ask Fink:

1. BlackRock's largest holdings include the most successful corporations in the world. How did these corporations become so successful without benefiting their stakeholders?
2. How did these corporations collectively achieve trillions of dollars in revenues without benefiting their customers?
3. How did these corporations come to employ millions of people without benefiting their employees?

Senator Elizabeth Warren and the Accountable Capitalism Act

Senator Elizabeth Warren (D-MA) used the stakeholder fallacy to promote one of her regulatory proposals, the Accountable Capitalism Act. It's an interesting title. Accountable to whom?

Capitalism means that people freely choose with whom they trade. Stakeholders and firms are accountable to each other. An employer and an employee are accountable to each other. The employer promises wages and benefits; the employee pledges time and effort. Both sides are free to walk away from the deal if they are unhappy with the terms or if they feel the other is not keeping its side of the bargain. The same is true for a firm's customers and its suppliers.

Here is an excerpt from a *Wall Street Journal* article in which Senator Warren discusses a motivation for this act. She invokes the stakeholder fallacy and implies that when a firm makes a profit, only the shareholders benefit:

> American corporations exist only because the American people grant them charters. Those charters confer valuable privileges—such as limited legal liability for their owners—that enable businesses to turn a profit. What do Americans get in return? What are the obligations of corporate citizenship in the U.S.?[17]

What do Americans get in return when firms are profitable? Businesses that earn profits do so by making their stakeholders better off. Profits reflect mutually beneficial trading. Employees get jobs they value, customers get goods and services they value, suppliers get to make profits, and governments collect taxes. Profits also encourage firms to make the best use of society's scarce resources. A profit reflects the fact that a firm has used resources that are of relatively low value to society to create goods or services that are of higher value to society. That is what Americans get in return.

Senator Warren suggests that corporate charters *enable* firms to earn profits. So, if there were no corporate charters, businesses could not earn profits? Business and commerce have existed for all of recorded history, long before the modern corporation emerged. The archaeological evidence discussed in the Introduction suggests that trading has been going on for at least 300,000 years.

A corporate charter does not guarantee that a firm will earn a profit. As mentioned in Chapter 1, most new firms go on to make losses. Twenty percent of new businesses do not survive the first year. Less than half survive five years. The 10-year survival rate is about 33 percent.[18] Corporations that earn consistent profits are the exception, not the rule.

Senator Warren points out that charters grant a business owner limited liability. Limited liability means that shareholders' losses are limited to their investment in the business. If you are a shareholder in a company and it goes bankrupt, the value of your investment goes to zero, but your personal assets are not at risk. If a creditor is not fully repaid after the company is liquidated, the creditor cannot come after your personal assets, such as your home or savings. Creditors know this and take it into account when they lend.

If we did not have limited liability, fewer people would be willing to invest in businesses, given the risk of losing personal assets. Fewer businesses mean fewer goods and services, less choice in goods and services, less competition, and higher prices. It means fewer jobs, less innovation, and less economic growth. Limited liability therefore benefits all of society, not just business owners.[19]

The Accountable Capitalism Act suggests that successful corporations don't consider the interests of their stakeholders, and the act is needed to rectify the situation:

> American corporations with more than $1 billion in annual revenue must obtain a federal charter from a newly formed Office of United States Corporations at the Department of Commerce. The new federal charter obligates company directors to consider the interests of all corporate stakeholders—including employees, customers, shareholders, and the communities in which the company operates.[20]

The Act targets successful firms, with $1 billion in annual revenue. How did these firms become successful without considering the interests of all stakeholders? I would like to ask Senator Warren the same type of questions that I would ask the Business Roundtable CEOs and Larry Fink.

1. Why do customers choose to buy so much in goods and services from these firms?
2. Why do employees choose to work for these firms?
3. Why do local communities tolerate and often seek to attract these firms?

It is not possible to build a $1 billion business without considering the interests of all stakeholders. Firms have to interact repeatedly with customers, employees, suppliers, lenders, and regulators. Each of these parties must be willing to transact with the firm, year after year, for the firm to be profitable over the long run. Firms that ignore their stakeholders' interests go out of business.

Harvard Business Review

Some of the strongest promoters of the stakeholder fallacy work at leading universities. The *Harvard Business Review* is a popular outlet for articles, often penned by academics, that criticize shareholder capitalism and promote various alternatives. This quote from the editor, Adi Ignatius, is an example of how so many in academia fail to understand that a firm's profit is largely determined by the well-being of its stakeholders:

> Financial performance should no longer be the sole pursuit of the corporation. Companies are being pushed to consider the interests of all their stakeholders—including employees, customers, and the community—not just those of their shareholders.[21]

Financial performance metrics are usually driven by profits and therefore reflect transactions that benefit the firm's other stakeholders. It is not just currently that companies are "being pushed to consider the interests of all their stakeholders," as Ignatius wrote. Companies have always had to consider the interests of their other stakeholders. Otherwise, they would not make profits and would go out of business. This is a basic fact of capitalism. Stakeholders will not transact with a company unless it serves their interests. This has always been the case.

Ignatius also mentions the "community"—a vague term that shareholder capitalism critics like to invoke. Who gets to speak for the community? Is it some academic or social responsibility activist who claims to speak for the greater good, or is it the people who live and work there? Many of the stakeholders who benefit from trading with a firm—employees, customers, and suppliers—live in the area or "community" where the firm operates. So, the "community" benefits in that respect. Firms are regulated by federal, state, and local governments, all of which are elected by the "community." A firm exists and thrives to the extent that government regulations allow it to trade with stakeholders who wish to trade with it. That all should encompass any definition of "the community."

9

SHAREHOLDER CAPITALISM VERSUS STAKEHOLDER CAPITALISM

To whom would corporate managers end up being accountable in a stakeholder-centric world? There are an uncountable number of stakeholders. In such a world, could managers ever be accused of making a wrong decision? If I as a manager justified a corporate decision as serving the interests of the workers, or the community or the Metropolitan Opera, how could my decision ever be challenged? The focus on shareholders is what gives you much clearer accountability.[1]

—*Glenn Hubbard*

In shareholder capitalism, a stakeholder is not expected to trade with a firm unless it benefits the stakeholder. If an employee does not find it to her benefit to work for a firm, she can choose to not work there. If a customer does not find it to his benefit to buy a product or service, he is under no obligation to do so. If a supplier does not find a relationship with a counterparty profitable, it is free to end it. By the same token, firms are not expected to trade with these stakeholders unless it benefits the shareholders. If a relationship with an employee, a customer, or a supplier does not benefit the shareholders, the firm ought to end it.

Employees, suppliers, customers, and other stakeholders look out for their own interests when they decide to transact with a firm. The majority of shareholders, however, aren't present when a large corporation makes most of its business decisions. They hire the CEO and other managers to make decisions on their behalf. If business managers enter arrangements with stakeholders that come at the expense of shareholders, then they aren't practicing capitalism. Transferring wealth from one stakeholder to another, benefiting one party at the other's expense, is not capitalism. It is not mutually beneficial. There is no value being created.

So, what is stakeholder capitalism? We have two possibilities.

1. Stakeholder capitalism is the same thing as shareholder capitalism, and its promoters are confused about what shareholder capitalism is. For example, the previous chapter quoted Larry Fink, who characterized stakeholder capitalism as consisting of "mutually beneficial" relations between a firm and its other stakeholders. This description is no different from shareholder capitalism.

2. Stakeholder capitalism is an oxymoron. Klaus Schwab and the Business Roundtable CEOs don't discuss mutual benefits when they describe stakeholder capitalism. This omission leaves the door open for managers to use the firm's resources for causes that don't benefit the shareholders. Wealth can be taken from shareholders and given to other stakeholders. Such transfers of wealth are not part of capitalism, which is characterized by mutually beneficial exchanges.

Putting Customers First

Some critics of shareholder capitalism point to a particular group of stakeholders, such as employees or customers, and argue that this stakeholder group ought to come first. It is worth exploring these arguments in more detail, as they can lead to absurd outcomes. You may have heard the mantra that "the customer comes first." This idea was promoted by management professor and author Peter Drucker. In his highly cited book, *The Practice of Management*, Drucker wrote "There is only one valid definition of business purpose: *to create a customer.*"[2]

Drucker had a point; a firm cannot exist without customers who willingly buy its products. There is nothing about shareholder capitalism that contradicts this fact. But meeting the needs of customers cannot be the primary purpose of a business, as we can easily have scenarios in which the customer's needs are met and the business is destroyed. Not every customer is a good one, and not every customer demand should be met.

If firms were to literally put their customers first and ignore all other considerations, they would do absurd things, like sell products below cost or even give products away for free. This would meet the needs of customers and attract many new customers. But it would come at the expense of the shareholders. Under such pricing schemes, management would be giving the company's—that is, the shareholders'—wealth away to customers. Do enough of this, and soon there is no business left.

The CEO's job is to maximize shareholder value by creating profits. This entails meeting the needs of customers, but is different from putting the customers first. If meeting customers' needs does not result in profits, then there is no business.

Putting Employees First

Should the firm put its employees first?

If a business's primary goal is to make employees happy, it can double wages, cut employees' responsibilities in half, or both. That would make employees happy. But it would come at the expense of the shareholders. If businesses do enough of this, wages consume all the profits, and there is no business.

Again, the corporate manager's job is to make a profitable business. That entails meeting the needs of employees, but it is different from putting the employees first.

Firms can make valuable investments in employees that benefit both employees and shareholders. Higher wages can incentivize employees to do better work. The value of such work may offset the increase in wages. But if increasing wages is not offset by an increase in productivity or some other source of value creation, then you don't increase wages. Doing so would transfer wealth from the shareholders to the employees.

Some pundits have argued that the employees of various firms ought to be paid more, regardless of any corresponding benefits to shareholders.[3] That view is the same as arguing that wealth should be transferred from one group of people—the shareholders—to another group of people—the employees. Those who argue that a particular group of employees ought to be paid more are not offering the employees better-paying jobs. Instead, they are making statements about how the shareholders' money ought to be spent. Employees work at a firm because the compensation and work environment are better than what any other enterprise is offering them, or they would work at that other enterprise.

Is the CEO an Employee or a Philosopher-King?

In shareholder capitalism, it is recognized that the firm belongs to the shareholders and that the CEO and other managers work for the shareholders. The CEO is an employee. The CEO's job is not to conduct a philosophical exercise in which he divvies up the firm's profits among the various stakeholders. The firm's profits, which result from transactions that have made the firm's other stakeholders better off, belong to the shareholders. The CEO's job is to ensure that the firm's resources are used to maximize shareholder value.

In stakeholder capitalism, things are less clear. The CEO is accountable to everyone, and therefore to no one. In Figure 9.1,

Figure 9.1. The company at the center point of its stakeholders

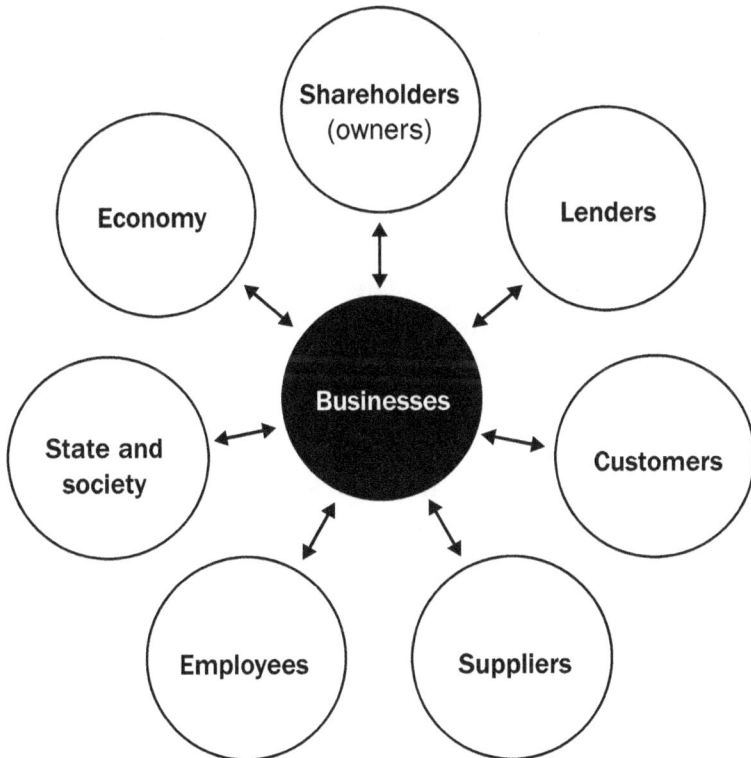

Source: Klaus Schwab and Hein Kroos, *Modern Company Management in Mechanical Engineering* (Frankfurt, Germany: Verein Deutscher Maschinenbau-Anstalten e.V., 1971), reproduced at "What Is Stakeholder Capitalism?," World Economic Forum website, January 22, 2021.

a diagram by Klaus Schwab, the business is in the middle, and the shareholders are just another stakeholder that the CEO deals with. It is easy to see why some CEOs like stakeholder capitalism. It effectively gives them license to do whatever they want with resources that do not belong to them. For almost any decision, it can be argued that some stakeholder benefited. The CEO is then no longer just an employee but a philosopher-king who has carte blanche with the firm's resources.

Capitalism Means No Zero-Sum Games

In a market economy, both parties get to freely choose if they interact with one another. A gain by one side is not matched with a loss on the other side. Nothing is forced, and both sides can benefit from a transaction. For a firm to survive and prosper, it needs to figure out a business plan in which both the shareholders and the other stakeholders benefit. This is the same as stating that the firm needs a plan that creates profits.

The following statements will be true for a profitable firm creating wealth for its shareholders.

- Customers buy the firm's products because the value that the customer places on the products meets or exceeds the sale price. Correspondingly, the sale price of the product exceeds the firm's costs by a large enough margin such that the firm makes a sufficient profit.
- Employees work at the firm because what it offers them is better than what any other enterprise—or unemployment—offers them. By the same token, the value of an employee's work to the firm meets or exceeds what the firm gives to the employee in compensation.
- Suppliers sell their products to the firm because the sale price creates a sufficient profit for the supplier. The firm

buys the suppliers' products because it can use them to create a new product that makes the firm a sufficient profit.

That is shareholder capitalism. Both shareholders and the other stakeholders benefit; otherwise, there are no transactions, no profits, and no firm.

Do both sides in a transaction benefit in stakeholder capitalism? Are transactions that transfer wealth from shareholders to other stakeholders permitted under stakeholder capitalism? Do parties not directly involved in the transaction have a say in it? Schwab and other proponents of stakeholder capitalism claim that everyone benefits but don't offer any decision rules. Instead, you get illustrations like Figure 9.1, which is posted on the World Economic Forum's website.[4]

This illustration does not tell us how to resolve conflicts among the parties. Employees want higher wages. Customers want lower prices. Suppliers want higher prices. In shareholder capitalism, there is an explicit rule that you do not harm the shareholders. You do not agree to schemes that transfer wealth from shareholders to other stakeholders. If stakeholder capitalism allows for schemes that transfer wealth from shareholders to other stakeholders, then it isn't capitalism. If stakeholder capitalism does not allow for such schemes and requires that shareholders benefit from each transaction, then it is the same thing as shareholder capitalism.

Furthermore, the diagram is inaccurate in that it suggests that shareholders and other stakeholders are trading with something called "businesses." Businesses are not tangible entities that just pop into existence and begin trading with people. A business does not trade with its shareholders. To the contrary, the business's owners—in a corporation, they are called shareholders—trade with the other stakeholders—employees, suppliers, customers, and lenders. We call that trading activity a business. It is a part of the economy and is regulated and taxed by the state.

Zero-Sum Games Are Shortsighted

Critics of shareholder capitalism see a company like Apple. It has billions of dollars in cash. It does not need to raise capital by issuing shares. And the critics say, "What's the problem with not maximizing shareholder value? Why not use Apple's assets for other causes? Why not distribute Apple's cash to other stakeholders we like better? Who cares if Apple's shareholders have a few dollars less?"

The problem with this line of reasoning is that Apple began as a small firm that did not have cash, did not make profits, and needed to issue shares. It was able to raise capital via an IPO because the IPO price reflected the possibility that it might become the successful business it is today, and the resulting cash flow and profit would belong to the shareholders. If Apple had been expected instead to distribute any profits it might generate among a nebulous group of "stakeholders," there likely would have been no IPO—and none of the MacBooks, iPhones, iPads, or any of the company's other products that many people enjoy today. Would you invest in a business in which failure means you take the loss and success means others get the gains?

Venture capital (VC) firms bought shares in Apple years before its IPO, back when it was still being run out of a garage.[5] The price the VCs paid for the shares reflected the fact that, if successful, Apple might launch an IPO, and the VCs' shares would gain significantly in value. Before the VC funding, Apple founders Steve Jobs and Steve Wozniak knew that if their long-shot business showed promise, they could attract a VC firm and perhaps go public at some point.

It is the possibilities of VC funding and IPOs that encourage some entrepreneurs to take risks and start businesses. If we decide to buy into the notion that corporate managers or some undefined group of "stakeholders" can use the assets of successful companies for purposes that do not benefit the shareholders, then we should expect less entrepreneurship, less VC funding, and fewer IPOs. We should expect a less innovative and more stagnant economy. Playing zero-sum games with Apple's shareholders limits the funding for the next generation of risky yet promising companies.

10

THE SHORT-TERM FALLACY

A company's shareholders prefer to be rich rather than poor. Therefore, they want the firm to invest in every project that is worth more than it costs. The difference between a project's cost and its value is its net present value (NPV). Companies can best help their shareholders by investing in all projects with a positive NPV and rejecting all projects with a negative NPV.[1]

—*Richard Brealey, Stewart Myers, Franklin Allen, and Alex Edmans*

The above quote is from a popular finance textbook commonly used in Finance 101 courses at universities around the world. The quote summarizes the investment policy that a firm should follow under shareholder capitalism. I also discussed the NPV rule in Chapter 2 of this book. Shareholder value is maximized by accepting all projects in which the value created exceeds the cost. Hundreds of finance professors teach the NPV rule to thousands of students every year, and we have been doing so for decades. It is also common sense. A business owner who has never taken a university finance course tries to do as much.

There is a fallacy that I call the short-term fallacy. It is based on the false claim that shareholder capitalism encourages managers to focus on short-term profits at the expense of long-term growth. A firm can make its short-term profits higher by investing less. The short-term fallacy implies that doing so benefits shareholders. This view is completely wrong. Perhaps the promoters of this fallacy have not taken Finance 101 and don't know how to value a business. They know that profits matter but then mistakenly think that short-term profits matter most. Yet the value of a business has little to do with short-term profits and a lot to do with growth in profits over the long run.

A positive NPV investment usually trades lower profits today for greater profits in the future. Positive NPV investment is consistent with shareholder capitalism and the goal of maximizing shareholder value. Firms make such investments all the time.

Klaus Schwab and the World Economic Forum

Klaus Schwab and the WEF have promoted both the short-term fallacy and the stakeholder fallacy (discussed in Chapter 8) for decades. In that regard, it can be said that no organization has done more to undermine financial literacy than the WEF. Here are a few examples of Schwab and the WEF promoting the idea that shareholder capitalism encourages firms to focus on short-term profits at the expense of everything else.

In a 2020 *Time* magazine article, Schwab wrote the following:

> Rather than chasing short-term profits or narrow self-interest, companies could pursue the well-being of all people and the entire planet. . . . The initial idea that companies should try and optimize for more than just short-term profits came around 2016 from a handful of business leaders who wanted the private sector to play a role in achieving the U.N. Sustainable Development Goals (SDGs).[2]

Schwab's 2021 book *Stakeholder Capitalism* proposes a "third way," with the first and second being shareholder capitalism and government-owned businesses. A WEF press release promoting Schwab's book provided the following description:

> Schwab proposes a third way: the model of stakeholder capital-
> ism. It is one where companies seek long-term value creation
> instead of short-term profits.[3]

In the book, Schwab writes:

> We can't continue with an economic system driven by selfish
> values, such as short-term profit maximization.[4]

Compare all this with the quote from the Finance 101 text-book at the top of this chapter. There is no economic framework, be it shareholder capitalism or any other, that says firms should optimize for short-term profits at the expense of value creation or longer-term success. Shareholder capitalism requires firms to accept all positive NPV projects, which is the opposite of what Schwab is claiming.

An article on stakeholder capitalism by Schwab, which is also quoted from in the previous chapter, contains the short-term fallacy and the stakeholder fallacy in a single sentence:

> That is the core of stakeholder capitalism: it is a form of cap-
> italism in which companies do not only optimize short-term
> profits for shareholders, but seek long term value creation, by
> taking into account the needs of all their stakeholders, and
> society at large.[5]

This quote could also describe shareholder capitalism. In shareholder capitalism, firms do not optimize for short-term profits. Firms seek to create shareholder value by entering into mutually beneficial exchanges with customers, suppliers, and employees. Firms make profits by using resources on which society places a relatively low value on and creating goods and services on which society places a higher value.

A couple of these quotes by the WEF and Schwab are inconsistent with one another. The second quote states that stakeholder capitalism promotes "long-term value creation *instead of* short-term profits" (emphasis added). The fourth quote states that, under stakeholder capitalism, firms "*not only* optimize short-term profits for shareholders, but seek long term value creation" (emphasis added). So, which ist it? Does stakeholder capitalism promote long-term profits over short-term profits, or does it allow for both? This inconsistency highlights a problem with stakeholder capitalism (and corporate social responsibility in general), which is that it is so poorly defined that even its proponents cannot articulate what its rules are.

The European Commission and Ernst & Young

In 2020, the European Commission, the European Union's executive branch, commissioned EY (formerly Ernst & Young) to help it promote its notion of stakeholder capitalism. It is largely motivated by the short-term fallacy. Here is how the report begins:

> The focus of corporate decision-makers on short-term shareholder value maximisation rather than on the long-term interests of the company reduces the long-term economic, environmental and social sustainability of European businesses.[6]

The report goes on to say:

> Directors' duties and company's interest are interpreted narrowly and tend to favour the short-term maximisation of shareholder value.[7]

And provides this statement:

> Growing pressures from investors with a short-term horizon contribute to increasing the boards' focus on short-term financial returns to shareholders at the expense of long-term value creation.[8]

A group of professors affiliated with the European Corporate Governance Institute wrote a response to the EY report. The response has 81 signatories, including many who are finance professors at leading universities:

> The policy debate has also been framed by reference to "short-term shareholder value". Yet, shareholder value is by definition a long-term concept—it is the present value of all future cash flows. This is true in practice, not just theory: many of the world's most valuable companies derive their worth from their growth opportunities, not their current profits. A company can only create shareholder value if it invests for the long-term.[9]

That's correct; there is no such thing as "short-term shareholder value." There is only one shareholder value, and it is largely a function of long-term profits. This is straight out of Finance 101. Every undergraduate textbook says as much.

Also responding to the EY report, London Business School finance professor Alex Edmans explained:

> The study repeatedly refers to "short-term shareholder value". This is an oxymoron because shareholder value is an inherently long-term concept.[10]

The WEF makes a similar statement about "near-term value creation" and shareholders in its Davos Manifesto 2020, which supposedly teaches us "The Universal Purpose of a Company in the Fourth Industrial Revolution." Here is a statement from the manifesto:

> A company provides its shareholders with a return on investment that takes into account the incurred entrepreneurial risks and the need for continuous innovation and sustained investments. It responsibly manages near-term, medium-term and long-term value creation in pursuit of sustainable shareholder returns that do not sacrifice the future for the present.[11]

There are no such things as "near-term, medium-term, and long-term value creation." I have been teaching finance for almost 20 years and I never heard these terms until I began doing research for this book. There is only a single firm value, the value today, and it reflects the firm's future profits. The way to maximize shareholder value is by accepting all positive NPV projects. The shareholder's holding period is irrelevant. Whether the shareholder plans to hold the stock for one year, five years, or 20 years, it is the same. Value for all shareholders is maximized by investing in positive NPV projects and avoiding negative NPV projects. A corporate manager who is trying to maximize shareholder value does not have different value-creation strategies for different shareholders based on expected holding periods.

The Harvard Law School Forum on Shareholder Capitalism

In 2021, Harvard Law School hosted a forum on shareholder capitalism. One of the participants was attorney Martin Lipton, a founding partner of the New York law firm Wachtell, Lipton, Rosen & Katz, the most profitable law firm in the world. Wachtell advises firms on mergers and acquisitions and other matters related to corporate strategy and governance.

Lipton, an advocate of stakeholder capitalism, said the following at the forum:

> It was sort of given that a company should be managed in order to maximize value for shareholders, but maximizing value evolved into a set of short-termist corporate policies and practices, which pressures and incentivizes management to drive up profits, regardless of longer-term costs, and has allowed activists to use the guise of good governance to reap quick and handsome profits.[12]

Responding to Lipton, another panelist at the forum, Cliff Asness, a money manager and founder of AQR Capital Management (and a finance PhD), said:

> Let me start by saying that I am puzzled by that argument. If management is trying to maximize short-term profits, those short-term benefits must come at the expense of long-term profits; and in a reasonably efficient stock market, that would have to be bad for the stock price, right? Management would be failing to invest in or build their businesses. So, how would that reflect a focus on shareholder value? . . . I have never gotten an answer to that question.[13]

Asness has good reason to be skeptical of the claim that skipping valuable investments can increase stock prices. Lipton claims that managers increase both short-term profits and stock prices by cutting valuable investments. Yet these investments were valuable, so the firm is now worth less. Thus, according to Lipton's statement, the firm is worth less *and* stock prices go up. How can that be?

Pump-and-Dump Schemes

Lipton and other proponents of the short-term fallacy argue that firms are under pressure to meet Wall Street's expectations about quarterly earnings and will cut back on investments to do so. To the extent that this happens, the managers' actions are inconsistent with shareholder capitalism. The rule in shareholder capitalism is found in the quote at the beginning of this chapter: Make all investments for which the value of what is created exceeds the cost. End of story.

Why might stock prices fall if a firm's earnings are less than what Wall Street analysts expect? A firm's value is based on all its expected future profits. After seeing a lower-than-expected profit number, some investors may lower their *forecasts of future profits*, thereby reducing the firm's value and the stock price. If this is the firm's economic reality, then so be it. The corporate manager's job is not to fool investors into believing that a business is more profitable than it is. That would be a type of fraud. And although fraud happens, it is not part of shareholder capitalism, which advocates mutually beneficial exchange, not one party taking advantage of another.

Let's assume that firms can dupe investors by cutting positive NPV investment and boosting short-term earnings. In this setting, a firm cuts its investment and investors don't realize that the higher earnings today came at the expense of skipping positive NPV investments. Investors then place too high an expectation on future profits. The stock price is then inflated. Eventually, investors will realize that the firm's earnings are not growing as fast as expected, and the stock price will deflate.

This scenario is a type of "pump-and-dump" scheme. The price is "pumped" up by the inflated earnings, and investors in the know sell or "dump" their shares before others figure out that the earnings are inflated and the share price is too high. Such schemes *do not create shareholder wealth*. Rather, they *transfer wealth* from the new shareholders who buy the inflated shares to the previous shareholders who sell the inflated shares.

If reducing investment to increase earnings *temporarily* inflates stock prices, shareholders can gain only if they sell their inflated shares before the price corrects and the inflation subsides. Those who buy the inflated shares become shareholders, and when the price eventually deflates, they take a loss on their investment. The loss of the new shareholders is precisely equal to the gain of the old shareholders who sold them the inflated shares. Moreover, skipping the positive NPV investment makes the firm less valuable, and the shareholders who didn't sell their shares, who are likely the vast majority, poorer.

Shareholder capitalism encourages the *creation of wealth*, not the *transfer of wealth* from one group of shareholders to another via deceptive means. And it certainly doesn't encourage skipping out on positive NPV investments.

Pump-and-dump schemes are inconsistent with the principles Milton Friedman laid out in his 1970 *New York Times Magazine* article, which some point to as the origin of shareholder capitalism.

> There is one and only one social responsibility of business—to use its resources and engage in activities designed to increase its profits so long as it stays within the rules of the game, which is to say, engages in open and free competition without deception or fraud.[14]

How often do these types of schemes happen? Are corporate managers able to inflate stock prices by cutting investment and boosting earnings? There is a good deal of empirical research on this, and it does not support the idea that when firms report high earnings numbers, they have inflated stock prices. It's actually the opposite. There is much evidence that investors undervalue firms with high levels of profits and overvalue more speculative firms that make large investments and are expected to grow rapidly. There are numerous studies documenting these effects.[15] I'll discuss the findings toward the end of the next chapter.

11

DO SHAREHOLDERS HAVE A SHORT-TERM FOCUS?

There continues today to be much criticism of U.S. companies as too short-term oriented and not oriented enough towards innovation. Those criticisms are not new. They have a long history that goes back at least thirty-five years. If the short-term orientation were true and such a bad thing, its effects should have shown up by now. But none of those effects have appeared.[1]

—*Steven Kaplan*

The short-term fallacy takes a dim view of shareholders and potential shareholders. It envisions shareholders as being myopic, focused only on what is right in front of them, and oblivious to basic finance. Shareholders are so focused on the short term, the thinking goes, that they fail to recognize how today's investments create long-term value.

Does this argument have any merit? Do shareholders really overvalue short-term profits and ignore long-run growth?[2] Of course, some of them do. There are thousands of publicly traded companies and millions of shareholders, so we can find anecdotes for almost anything. But does the typical shareholder behave this way? That would be surprising. Virtually every business school student takes a Finance 101 course on how to value a business. Professional fund managers have taken Finance 101 and have professional training and experience on how to value a business. They also largely determine stock prices. Institutional investors account for 90 percent of the trading volume and 78 percent of the ownership of Russell 3000 stocks, which are the 3,000 largest publicly traded companies.[3]

But what does the evidence say? Is the average investor oblivious to Finance 101? I'll start with a couple of examples to provide a better understanding of how shareholders value long-term growth. Then I will move on and discuss the empirical evidence.

A Thought Experiment with Pfizer

As mentioned in Chapter 2, Pfizer spent almost $14 billion on R&D investments in 2021, which lowered its profits by the same amount. Would Pfizer's shareholders be better off if it had cut all its R&D spending and had $14 billion more in profits?

In June 2022, Pfizer's market capitalization was $270 billion. Its profits in 2021 were $21.98 billion, less than 10 percent of its market capitalization. Why were shareholders willing to pay $270 billion for a company with $21.98 billion in profits?

Pfizer's shareholders own Pfizer's future profits, to be earned in 2024, 2030, 2040, and so on. Pfizer's stock price and market capitalization are based on these expected profits. Much of those future profits will be created by today's R&D spending.

The $14 billion in R&D spending likely makes Pfizer's stock price higher. Pfizer's executives and shareholders expect these R&D investments to lead to new drugs, which will in turn generate future profits that will more than offset the $14 billion investment. Put differently, Pfizer is making positive NPV investments. Pfizer's shareholders understand this; they studied basic finance and know how to value a business. The expected future profits from the $14 billion R&D investment are reflected in Pfizer's stock price today.

If Pfizer were to cut its R&D spending to increase near-term profits, its stock price would likely fall. Shareholders would recognize that Pfizer would be killing a big portion of its future business, which is based on developing new drugs. The short-term fallacy suggests that shareholders are too ignorant to realize this tradeoff. If that is so, then why did Pfizer spend the $14 billion? Why did Merck spend $12.2 billion on its R&D? Why did Johnson & Johnson spend $14.7 billion? Why did AstraZeneca spend $9.7 billion?[4]

Why Was Elon Musk the Richest Man in the World in 2022?

According to *Forbes*, Elon Musk was the richest man in the world in 2022, with a net worth of $219 billion.[5] Musk's wealth reflects his ownership in Tesla, which is a publicly traded company, and SpaceX, which is a private company. Both companies have small earnings and revenues compared to their equity values. The value of both companies, and Musk's net worth, is driven by shareholders placing a high value on expected long-term growth, not near-term profits.

Tesla ended its fiscal year 2021 with a market capitalization of $1.061 trillion and profits of $5.5 billion. As a comparison, Ford Motor Company ended 2021 with profits of $17.9 billion and a market capitalization of $83 billion. Ford had more than triple the profits of Tesla, but Tesla had more than 12 times the market capitalization of Ford. Why are shareholders willing to pay $1.061 trillion for a company that had profits of only $5.5 billion? Table 11.1 shows that shareholders were willing to pay $192.91 per $1 of profit to own Tesla stock but only $4.80 per $1 of profit to own Ford stock. Why the difference?

Table 11.1

Profit and market capitalization for Tesla and Ford, end of 2021 fiscal year

	Tesla ($)	Ford ($)
Profits	5.5 billion	17.9 billion
Market capitalization	1.061 trillion	86 billion
Market capitalization per $1 profit	192.91	4.80

Source: Stockanalysis.com.

The answer is that shareholders have a claim to all of the firm's future profits. Therefore, a major determinant of value is *how much profits are expected to grow*. Shareholders believe the future is brighter for Tesla than for Ford. They expect Tesla's profits to grow faster than—and eventually overtake—Ford's. That's why shareholders are willing to pay so much more, in terms of current profits, to own a share of Tesla. Stock prices reflect expectations of growth.

Tesla spent about $2.6 billion in R&D in 2021, about half of its total profits. Would Tesla's stock price be higher if it eliminated its R&D spending and increased its profits by the same amount? No, that would likely cause its stock price to fall. Tesla's future growth depends on its ability to innovate. Shareholders know this, and they price its stock accordingly.

SpaceX is a private company, but Musk is not the only owner. He has sold shares to other investors. Based on what those investors paid for their shares, SpaceX had a value of $74 billion in 2021.[6] SpaceX's *sales* were only $1.6 billion in 2021. Why would investors pay $74 billion to own a company that only has $1.6 billion in sales? They are betting on SpaceX's future. SpaceX is a long-term bet.

If investors were shortsighted and unwilling to make long-term bets, there would be no SpaceX, no Tesla, and no innovative start-ups for that matter.

Initial Public Offerings

Chapter 5 discussed the funding of highly innovative firms and provided statistics for U.S. IPOs. Often highly innovative firms are young, incurring high development costs, and without a finished product. Yet these firms can be worth millions or even billions of dollars. The statistics from Chapter 5 show that, over the past 40 years, the majority of technology and biotechnology IPO firms had negative profits. Over the last 20 years, 95 percent of biotech IPOs had negative profits and the majority had no revenues, meaning they did not have a finished product. Why would shareholders pay millions or even billions of dollars to own a part of these firms?

It is because shareholders expect these firms to generate significant profits in the future. When we value a business, we account for all its *expected future profits*. That is roughly what a stock price is. A stock price is an estimate of the present value of the firm's entire expected future cash flow, which is driven by expected future profits. This is why firms can lose money and still be worth millions or even billions of dollars. Shareholders therefore regularly invest billions into firms that are losing money with the hope of future profits and value creation.

Many of the IPOs over the past several decades turned out to be great investments, including Amazon, Microsoft, Moderna, and Tesla. Yet the evidence shows that on average, shareholders are too optimistic about the prospects of IPO firms. On average, IPOs have poor long-run returns, suggesting that investors are overly optimistic and pay too much for the shares of IPO firms.[7] Does that sound like a short-term focus to you?

Academic Studies on Mispriced Stocks

The short-term fallacy makes predictions that are testable. It claims that shareholders:

1. Place too much weight on short-term profits, and
2. Place too little weight on future growth created by investment.

According to proponents of the short-term fallacy, managers cut investment to increase profits, which in turn inflates stock prices. Stocks with inflated prices should have lower future stock returns as the inflation eventually subsides. Is there evidence of this? Do firms with high profits and low investment have low future stock returns?

Multiple studies find that firms with higher profits have higher future stock returns.[8] This finding suggests that highly profitable firms' stock prices might be *too low.* This is the opposite of what the short-term fallacy predicts.

Multiple studies also find that firms that make large capital investments have lower future stock returns.[9] This finding suggests that firms that make large investments have inflated stock prices. This result also contradicts the short-term fallacy, which claims that shareholders undervalue investment. Instead, it appears that investors overvalue investment. Why is this?

Research suggests that investors can be too optimistic about the future growth of fast-growing firms. As it becomes clear that such firms will not grow as fast as expected, the stock price falls. This is contrary to the short-term fallacy, which claims that shareholders place *too little* emphasis on future growth. If anything, shareholders are often *too optimistic* about potential growth in firms that have been growing fast and making large investments.

Tesla is the caricature of an overvalued firm. It has fast sales growth, high investment, and low profits relative to its market capitalization. Tesla has also raised a lot of capital. Each of these traits has been associated with lower future stock returns in published studies.[10] I'm not arguing that Tesla is overvalued. I'm stating that firms with these traits have had, on average, abnormally low stock returns. This has been the case both in the United States and internationally.

The caricature of an undervalued firm is the opposite of the caricature for an overvalued one.[11] It is the type of firm that Warren Buffett has tended to favor—a stable business in a mature, boring industry. The firm is profitable. It has produced steady, reliable profits and cash flow for some time. It pays dividends and repurchases shares. It is not raising capital. It is not making large investments. Its sales are not growing rapidly. Each of these traits have been shown to predict abnormally high stock returns.[12] The evidence suggests that investors tend to neglect such stocks in favor of something more exciting, like Tesla. Eventually, investors realize that the prices of these undervalued stocks are too low, so they buy the stocks, which pushes up their prices and creates the high stock returns.

12

THE INVESTMENT-GOOD/
PAYOUT-BAD FALLACY

In the department of economy, an act, a habit, an institution,
a law, gives birth not only to an effect, but to a series
of effects. Of these effects, the first only is immediate; it
manifests itself simultaneously with its cause—it is seen.
The others unfold in succession—they are not seen: it is
well for us, if they are foreseen. Between a good and a bad
economist this constitutes the whole difference—the one
takes account of the visible effect; the other takes account
both of the effects which are seen, and also of those which
it is necessary to foresee.[1]

—*Frederic Bastiat*

When firms generate profits, managers have a decision to make.
Do they reinvest in the firm or return the money to shareholders?
In shareholder capitalism, the rule is to maximize shareholder
value. This task is accomplished by investing in all positive NPV
projects. If no such projects exist, then excess funds should be
returned to shareholders. "Payout" is a term used to describe
returning funds to shareholders.

There are two payout mechanisms: cash dividends and share
repurchases. With dividends, the excess cash is divided by the

number of shares outstanding, and each shareholder receives a payment based on the number of shares owned. With repurchases, the cash is used to buy the firm's shares. The firm purchases its shares on the open market, the same way you and I would. After the repurchase, there are fewer shares outstanding, and the firm no longer holds the cash.

In Chapter 10, I discussed how the European Commission, the European Union's executive branch, commissioned a report from the consulting firm EY to help it study corporate "short-termism." The report focuses on a metric that is based on what I refer to as the investment-good/payout-bad fallacy. The report argues that short-termism can be measured by comparing payout to investment, with greater payout relative to investment reflecting greater short-termism. In justifying this metric, the report offers this explanation:

> The hypothesis underlining this approach is that companies decide to use their net income either to fund their shareholders, or to invest in future earnings. Therefore, the increasing payments to shareholders will decrease the available resources to invest, in R&D, human capital or other kinds of capital expenditures (CAPEX), thus jeopardising future productivity growth.[2]

This statement is so confused that it's hard to know where to begin to untangle it. Whether the firm decides to pay out or invest, everything ultimately comes back to the shareholders. Positive NPV investment means that if the firm invests, *shareholders are expected to have a larger payout in the future than today.* Investment creates future profits, which can be paid out to the shareholders in the future or invested in positive NPV projects. In the end, it all comes back to the shareholders.

Maximizing shareholder value *requires* the firm to invest in all positive NPV projects. A manager therefore first decides if the firm has positive NPV investments available to it. If it has none, then, and only then, should it make payouts to shareholders. It's Finance 101. Here is another quote from Chapter 1 of the popular textbook that I have used for years:

> A company developing renewable energy may be improving current shareholder wealth, even if the project is not profitable for 20 years.[3]

The investment-good/payout-bad fallacy is related to the short-term fallacy, which was covered in Chapter 10. Both fallacies claim that shareholder capitalism incentivizes firms to underinvest. Whereas the short-term fallacy claims that firms want to inflate stock prices by reporting higher profits, the investment-good/payout-bad fallacy claims that firms are inflating stock prices with payouts. Proponents of the investment-good/payout-bad fallacy have an especially strong dislike for share repurchases, which they believe inflate stock prices.

It is common for students new to finance to think that repurchases inflate the stock price. They eventually learn that repurchases do not inflate or have any mechanical effect on stock prices. This is Finance 102. I'll provide an example in the next chapter.

The statements made by the proponents of the investment-good/payout-bad fallacy suggest that they don't know how to value a business or what a positive NPV investment is. They recognize that payouts involve cash being transferred from the corporation to its shareholders, but they don't understand that payouts, done at the expense of a positive NPV investment, *harm shareholders*. Skipping positive NPV investments reduces the value of the business. It should lower the stock price, not inflate it.

People who argue that more investment is always better don't understand Economics 101. Investment benefits society only if the value of what is created exceeds the cost of the resources being used. Not all investment does that. Investment consumes scarce resources that have alternative uses. An investment that uses resources but does not create something of greater value harms society, since those resources could have been put to better use elsewhere. When firms pay out, the shareholders can invest the payout into different firms that have positive NPV investments.

Shareholder Capitalism and Payout: A Cheat Sheet

To clarify, here is what shareholder capitalism does say and does not say about investment and payout:

> *Does Say*: Accept all *positive* NPV investments. If the firm does not have enough capital to fund its investments, then it should issue shares or borrow.
>
> *Does Say*: Reject all negative NPV investments.
>
> *Does Say*: If the firm has excess cash and *no* positive NPV investments, then pay out to shareholders.
>
> *Does **Not** Say*: Reject positive NPV investments in favor of payout.

What Is Seen and What Is Unseen

The economist and philosopher Frederic Bastiat taught us 170 years ago that a good economist has to consider the unseen, as well as the seen effects of any action.[4] Proponents of the investment-good/payout-bad fallacy focus on the effects that are easy to see and ignore those that are more difficult to see.

Consider the following statement by Sen. Charles Schumer (D-NY):

> I hate stock buybacks. . . . I think they're one of the most self-serving things that Corporate America does instead of investing in workers and in training and in research and in equipment.[5]

With respect to buybacks or repurchases, the following effects are easy to see:

1. Cash was used to repurchase shares.
2. The firm could have instead invested the cash.

These effects are more difficult to see but just as important:

3. The fact that a firm chooses not to invest says something about its investment opportunities. Had the cash been invested, it likely would have gone to investments that destroyed value.
4. Cash being returned to shareholders can be invested elsewhere in the economy.

Senator Schumer focuses on the effects that are easy to see, but he ignores the ones that are not readily seen. It is not always better for firms to invest in training, R&D, or equipment. It can be the case that such investments create value, but it can also be the case that such investments destroy value. The corporate manager's job is to figure this out and invest accordingly. If we observe a firm paying out, chances are that the managers believe there are no positive NPV investments on which to spend that cash.

The World Economic Forum's Stakeholder Capitalism Metrics

The investment-good/payout-bad fallacy makes an appearance in the World Economic Forum's *Stakeholder Capitalism Metrics*. The metrics were developed in collaboration with Bank of America CEO Brian Moynihan and four major consulting firms, Deloitte, EY, KPMG, and PwC (formerly PriceWaterhouseCoopers). The metrics include investment, which is viewed as a positive, and payout, which is viewed as a negative. Here is what the description of the metrics tells us:

> Investment is a key driver of an economy's growth and a company's capacity to expand its operations and create additional employment. Wealth creation from investment activities can be evidenced through the company's expenditures to grow the business as compared to distribution of capital to shareholders.[6]

The authors of this statement seem to think that investment always creates value and that payout to shareholders cannot be reinvested to create value in different firms. In reality, investments can just as easily destroy value, while payout can be reinvested elsewhere.

Here are some questions I would like to ask Bank of America CEO Moynihan:

- Does Bank of America fund every business loan application that it receives? If not, why does it turn down some loan applications?
- Isn't it better for Bank of America to fund business loans only if it believes that the investments being funded will generate enough profits to pay back the loan with interest?
- If it's reasonable for Bank of America to discern good investments from bad ones, then shouldn't other firms do the same?

Taking the Fallacy Seriously

Let's try a new policy based on the investment-good/payout-bad fallacy. Every firm should invest as much as it can all the time. Invest, invest, invest, regardless of the value created. Boeing should build a new manufacturing facility to build planes, even if it does not have demand for those planes. Investment is good, so just make more planes. Don't worry about who will buy them. Starbucks should open as many stores as it can. Expand, expand, expand. Don't worry if those stores will generate enough profits to cover their costs. The goal is to open more stores. Pfizer should spend as much capital as it can on R&D for new drugs, regardless of whether the expected sales from those drugs will offset the cost of development. It is always good to invest. More is always better.

This investment policy would be bad for shareholders. If a firm invests $2 million and creates something that is worth $1 million, then the shareholders are poorer by $1 million. Will people continue to invest in firms if they pursue these types of policies? If firms follow such policies, will we in the long run have more firms or fewer firms?

Society would be worse off under the "invest more" policy. The land, labor, and capital used to build a plane, open a store, or develop a drug are scarce and have alternative uses. If those resources are used for projects that destroy value, then they cannot be used for different projects that create value. Society then gets fewer of the goods and services that it wants and needs and has surpluses of goods and services that it does not want or need. As discussed in Chapter 7, this was what happened in the Soviet Union, which eventually went bankrupt.

In the short run, "invest more" policies may create more jobs, but those jobs will not pay for themselves. If a firm pays people to create goods and services that do not generate profits, then the firm eventually runs out of money and then no firm or jobs remain. The irony here is that the critics of shareholder capitalism accuse it of short-termism, yet encouraging investment irrespective of value creation is the epitome of short-term thinking.

What Types of Firms Pay Out?

After a firm launches an IPO and its shares become publicly traded, it can continue to issue more shares. Most firms do so every year. The most common share issues are employee stock options.[7] The options give an employee the right to buy shares from the firm at a discounted price. When the employee exercises that option, new shares are issued. The firm gets cash and the employee gets shares of stock. Share repurchases are often just buybacks of shares that were issued during option exercises. So, we cannot make statements about repurchases and payout without accounting for share issues. *Net share issues* are calculated as follows:

Net Share Issues = Shares Issued − Share Repurchases

The largest share issues in dollar terms occur in stock-financed mergers, in which the acquiring firm issues shares to the shareholders of the firm being acquired.[8] Many studies leave these out when they estimate net share issues and then understate the propensity for firms to be positive net issuers.[9] If *net share issues* are measured correctly, then the majority of firms are positive net issuers, not net repurchasers.[10] This is true both in the United States and internationally.[11] The majority of publicly traded firms also do not pay dividends.[12]

Which types of firms are net repurchasers and dividend payers? Large, mature, profitable firms that have consistently had earnings larger than their investments.[13] These firms have excess cash that exceeds their investment opportunities, so they return it to their shareholders. Consistent with this finding, a comprehensive survey of 384 executives reports that "repurchases are made out of residual cash flow after investment spending."[14] Corporate managers are therefore largely in line with shareholder capitalism in this regard. Recent research also shows that repurchases increase stock liquidity and reduce volatility, thereby stabilizing stock prices, which also benefits shareholders.[15]

Which types of firms are positive net issuers and nonpayers of dividends? Smaller, younger, fast-growing firms tend to issue the most shares.[16] Firms with investment needs that exceed their profits. Firms that still have their greatest growth opportunities in front of them and are not yet producing reliable streams of profit, like the IPO firms discussed in the previous chapters.

Capital markets are largely working as they should. When firms have valuable investment opportunities but lack cash, they raise capital and invest. When firms have excess cash but lack valuable investment opportunities, they return the capital to their shareholders. The shareholders can then invest it elsewhere. This is as it should be.

Payout at Partnerships

A business can also be structured as a partnership. Like corporations, partnerships have payouts. Sens. Marco Rubio (R-FL), Charles Schumer (D-NY), and Elizabeth Warren (D-MA) are all critics of payouts at public corporations and especially repurchases. They also all have law degrees. Law firms are typically structured as partnerships. I have not heard any of these senators criticize law firms for distributing profits or buying out partners.

Partnerships divide profits among the partners, just as payouts at public corporations divide profits among shareholders. Partnerships also have buyouts, which are similar to share repurchases. A common buyout event is when a partner retires and the other partners buy out the retiree's share in the partnership.

As a case study, let's examine the most profitable law firm in the world, Wachtell, Lipton, Rosen & Katz.[17] As discussed in Chapter 10, the Lipton in this firm is Martin Lipton, the stakeholder capitalism advocate and shareholder capitalism critic. In 2020, Wachtell's profit per equity partner was estimated to be $7.5 million.[18] Why aren't the senators angry at Wachtell's partners for paying out its profits to themselves, rather than reinvesting back into the firm?

Wachtell has plenty of room to grow. Wachtell is one of the smallest firms on the Am Law 100, a ranking of the world's 100 most profitable law firms.[19] Some of Wachtell's peer law firms have multiple offices around the world, while Wachtell has only a single office in New York City. Why doesn't Wachtell invest more? Wachtell could open more offices. It could upgrade its office space. It could hire more lawyers. It could spend more on training its lawyers and other employees.

Perhaps these are all negative NPV investments, though, and Wachtell's partners are best served by its current size. In any case, if it's OK for Wachtell and other law firms to not grow and to pay out profits, then why can't publicly traded firms do the same? Why should Lipton be entitled to a multimillion-dollar payout, but not the shareholders of public corporations?

13

DO SHARE REPURCHASES INFLATE STOCK PRICES?

When you are told that all repurchases are harmful to shareholders or to the country, or particularly beneficial to CEOs, you are listening to either an economic illiterate or a silver-tongued demagogue (characters that are not mutually exclusive).[1]

—*Warren Buffett*

The investment-good/payout-bad fallacy is partly based on the idea that share repurchases inflate stock prices. Many prominent figures have claimed that firms use share repurchases as an illegitimate means to inflate stock prices. One very vocal critic of repurchases is Sen. Elizabeth Warren, who has described repurchases as "nothing but paper manipulation."[2] Sens. Chuck Schumer and Bernie Sanders (I-VT) are also critics. In a *New York Times* op-ed criticizing share repurchases, they wrote:

When a company purchases its own stock back, it reduces the number of publicly traded shares, boosting the value of the stock to the benefit of shareholders and corporate leadership.[3]

Although the senators quoted here are Democrats or, in Sanders's case, an Independent, this is not a partisan issue. The issue here is financial literacy and understanding the effects that share repurchases have on firm value and shareholders. The senators' logic seems to be that after a share repurchase, there are fewer shares outstanding, so each share should have a higher price. This line of reasoning overlooks the fact that the cash used to repurchase the shares is no longer held by the firm. Although it is true that the remaining shareholders own a greater share of the firm after the repurchase, the firm is also worth less, as it no longer holds the cash that was used to repurchase the shares. These two effects offset one another, so that the value of each share is unchanged. Yet this basic result, found in undergraduate textbooks and often taught in corporate finance courses, is not widely understood.

It is also curious that there is no criticism of share issues. If repurchasing shares is a type of "manipulation," then why isn't issuing shares "manipulation" as well? Both change the number of shares outstanding.

Share Repurchases at Private Corporations

Let's examine a simple repurchase at a private corporation and then walk through the repurchase process at a public corporation. You will see that the economics of repurchases are no different at a private corporation, a public corporation, or even a partnership such as a law firm. Decide for yourself if repurchases are a type of manipulation.

Consider a private corporation with two owners, you and me. The corporation owns a business and a bank account. The business is worth $90,000, and there is $10,000 in the bank account. The corporation is therefore worth $100,000. You own 90 percent of the corporation and I own 10 percent.

We agree that you will buy my share. You give me the $10,000 in the bank account in exchange for my 10 percent ownership.

Afterward, you own 100 percent of the corporation, which still owns the business, but none of the cash. The corporation is worth $90,000 now.

Your wealth did not change as a result of the repurchase. Before the repurchase, your share was 90 percent of a corporation that was worth $100,000, so your share was worth $90,000. After the repurchase, your share of the corporation is 100 percent, but the corporation is only worth $90,000. Your share was worth $90,000 before and after the repurchase. The value of your ownership was not changed by the repurchase. Similarly, my share was worth $10,000 before the repurchase, and I have $10,000 in cash after the repurchase. The repurchase had no effect on my wealth. See Table 13.1.

Table 13.1
Hypothetical example of a share repurchase at a private corporation

Before the Repurchase	
Business value	$90,000
Cash	$10,000
Total firm value	$90,000 + $10,000 = $100,000
Your ownership share	90% or $90,000
My ownership share	10% or $10,000
After the Repurchase	
Business value	$90,000
Cash	$0
Total firm value	$90,000 + $0 = $90,000
Your ownership share	100% or $90,000
My ownership share	0%
My cash	$10,000

Share Repurchase at Public Corporations

Now let's walk through a repurchase at a public corporation. A corporation owns a business and a bank account. The business has a value of $90 million. The bank account has $10 million.

- The corporation is worth $90 million + $10 million = $100 million.
- There are 10 million shares outstanding. Each share is worth $100 million/10 million = $10.
- The corporation's managers decide to use the $10 million of cash to repurchase shares.
- Each share is worth $10, so the corporation can repurchase $10 million/$10 = 1 million shares.
- After the repurchase, there are 10 million − 1 million = 9 million shares.

After the repurchase, the cash is gone and only the business remains. The value of the business is still $90 million. Each share is therefore worth $90 million/9 million = $10, the same as before the repurchase. See Table 13.2.

The shareholders who sold their shares back to the corporation no longer own part of the business, but they own the cash. The shareholders who kept their shares no longer own the cash, but they own more of the business. Neither group is better off or worse off. Compare that scenario with the following statement by the former secretary of labor Robert Reich (who is now a columnist and professor of public policy at the University of California, Berkeley):

> Stock buybacks are artificial efforts to interfere in the so-called "free market" to prop up stock prices. Because they create an artificial demand, they force stock prices above their natural level. With fewer shares in circulation, each remaining share is worth more.[4]

Do you see anything that resembles Reich's description here?

Table 13.2

Hypothetical example of a share repurchase at a public corporation

Before the Repurchase	
Business value	$90 million
Cash	$10 million
Total firm value	$90 million + $10 million = $100 million
Shares	10 million
Stock price	$100 million/10 million = $10
Shares to be repurchased	$10 million/$10 = 1 million
After the Repurchase	
Business value	$90 million
Cash	$0
Total firm value	$90 million + $0 = $90 million
Shares	10 million − 1 million = 9 million
Stock price	$90 million/9 million = $10

Repurchases and Stock Returns

The repurchase critics mentioned in this chapter suggest that repurchases inflate stock prices. Inflated stock prices should lead to low stock returns as the inflation subsides. Is this the case? Do firms that repurchase shares have low future stock returns?

No. The opposite is true. Firms that repurchase shares have high future stock returns. This is documented in multiple studies both in the United States and internationally.[5] When a firm announces a repurchase, there is usually a positive stock price reaction on the day of the announcement, followed by abnormally high returns over the following years. The first study to show this was published in 1995.[6] It's old news.

Why do repurchases predict higher stock returns? One explanation is that firms that engage in repurchases tend to be undervalued. Chapter 11 described the traits of firms that may be undervalued or neglected by investors. Such firms tend to be mature, and they consistently have high levels of profits relative to their investment needs. Several studies suggest that investors tend to ignore these firms in favor of newer, faster-growing, and more exciting firms.[7]

Executive Stock Options and Repurchases

Another criticism of repurchases is that executives time repurchases to coincide with their stock options exercises. When an employee stock option is exercised, the firm issues new shares to the employee. The employee then sells the shares on the stock market as you or I would. If the firm repurchases shares at the same time, there is more demand for the firm's shares, and the executives may be able to sell their shares at a higher price. There is evidence that some firms skip investments to engage in repurchases when executives exercise large amounts of stock options.[8]

If executives are skipping positive NPV investments in favor of repurchases, it is harmful to shareholders. Executives who engage in such actions contradict shareholder capitalism, while serving their own interests. Such actions are a type of "agency problem," in which the agents (executives) put their own interest ahead of the principals (shareholders) who employ them.

Finance professor Alex Edmans, who coauthored a well-known study showing that executive stock options are associated with repurchases, points out that such agency problems are not a reason to criticize or limit repurchases.[9] Rather, the problem that needs to be addressed is with the structure of some executive compensation packages that encourage these types of agency problems. Edmans also points out that the first-order reason for share repurchases is excess cash coupled with a lack of growth opportunities. The previous chapter discussed how it is well documented that firms that repurchase shares tend to be large, profitable firms that lack growth opportunities.[10]

As mentioned in the previous section, firms that repurchase shares tend to have abnormally high stock returns over the subsequent years. One study finds that the returns of repurchasers are 12.1 percent higher over the next four years compared with those of similar firms.[11] If repurchases primarily reflect agency problems and skipping valuable investments, then why do repurchasers have higher stock returns over the subsequent years?

Part Three

A CLOSER LOOK AT CORPORATE
SOCIAL RESPONSIBILITY

Part Three

14

CORPORATE GOVERNANCE

In this section, we take a closer look at corporate social responsibility and its effects on society. To understand how corporate social responsibility operates, we need to have a basic understanding of how corporations are governed.

If a business owner decides to incorporate her business, a new legal entity, the corporation, is created. Legally, the business's assets are owned by the corporation, not the business owner, but the business owner is given shares in the corporation. With these shares, the business owner can control the corporation and its assets and operate her business as she sees fit.

Potentially, there can be three different sets of persons in the governance structure of a corporation: the shareholders, the board of directors, and the management. Corporate shares come with voting rights, which enable the shareholders to vote on important policies and elect a board of directors. The board's job is to supervise the management on behalf of the shareholders. The board appoints the CEO and other executives and authorizes major decisions and policies, such as acquisitions, the sale of the corporation, and dividend payouts.

In the case of a privately held corporation, one person or small group of persons can play the roles of shareholders, board, and management. For example, Twitter recently went from being a publicly traded corporation to a private one owned by Elon Musk. Musk is now the owner, sole director, and CEO of Twitter.[1] After the purchase, Musk dissolved Twitter's board of directors, fired all the executives, terminated half the workforce, and began making major changes to the business's operations.[2] Musk clearly both owns and controls Twitter (which he recently renamed X).

Some critics of shareholder capitalism, such as attorney Martin Lipton, make the point that shareholders do not *own the corporation*; they *own shares in the corporation*.[3] The logic here seems to be based on the idea that a corporation is an independent legal entity that cannot be legally owned.[4] Lipton and others argue that since shareholders *do not own the corporation*, corporate managers don't have an obligation to maximize shareholder value.

Yet the corporation is essentially just a set of rules that govern the underlying business. The corporation exists on paper and in our imaginations and is real only to the extent that people agree to abide by its component rules. If a business is a corporation, and you own all of its shares, then you effectively own its assets.

For example, we can say that Elon Musk owns Twitter. Twitter has assets that are valuable. Elon Musk, and only Elon Musk, can use Twitter's assets for any purpose he wants. He can sell some or all of Twitter's assets. He has the exclusive right to Twitter's assets because he owns Twitter's shares. If the shares did not confer such rights, then Musk would not have paid $43 billion for them. Ironically, Twitter's former shareholders, who received the $43 billion, were represented by Martin Lipton's law firm.

Ownership and Control at Public Corporations

The issues concerning corporate social responsibility are concentrated in publicly traded corporations—those that have undergone

IPOs and have their shares traded on stock exchanges. This is because public corporations can have large separations between the persons who own the business—the shareholders—and those who control the business—the CEO and the other corporate managers.[5] The CEO and other managers may also be shareholders, but so are millions of other people. The shareholders are geographically dispersed, and the vast majority have no direct contact with the company's management. It is not possible for the shareholders to directly monitor the managers, who may want to use the firm's resources for their own agendas, rather than to maximize shareholder value.

To better understand how a public corporation is governed, we can compare it to a republic.[6] In a republic, politicians are elected by the people to supervise and direct the bureaucrats who run the various government agencies, which are supposed to serve the republic's citizens. Similarly, directors are elected by the shareholders to supervise the CEO and management team, to ensure that management's decisions create maximal value for the shareholders.

The governance of both corporations and republics is far from perfect. Politicians and government bureaucrats can put their own interests ahead of the people they are supposed to serve. The same can be said of corporate managers and directors. Elections and other mechanisms can limit such problems, but problems still exist.

Legally, corporate directors are fiduciary agents—persons designated to hold assets in trust, or to exercise authority on behalf of someone else. Directors have two main fiduciary duties, the *duty of care* and the *duty of loyalty*. The duty of care requires directors to make informed and reasonable decisions and exercise reasonable supervision of the business. The duty of loyalty requires directors to act in what they believe is the best interest of the corporation. That means no self-dealing; the corporation's welfare comes first. Directors should not exploit business opportunities that rightfully belong to the corporation for their own gain.

The *business judgment rule* gives directors a good deal of legal protection. It means that a court, unless given a good reason, will not second-guess a corporate board's business decisions. The assumption is that board members have acted in good faith and in line with their fiduciary duty. An aggrieved party must prove otherwise. This rule is similar to the legal presumption of innocence. The business judgement rule means that even if a business decision turns out to be wrong after the fact, it isn't subject to legal challenge unless, *in reaching the decision*, the board clearly sidestepped its fiduciary duties. Firms have to take risks, and risk taking sometimes will result in bad outcomes. If directors could be sued every time there was a bad outcome, then no one would want to serve as a company director.

Agency Problems and Expropriation

The separation of ownership and control at publicly traded corporations makes them prone to agency problems and expropriation. By expropriation, I mean the seizing or use of assets by someone other than their rightful owner without the rightful owner's consent. The people operating the corporation—the agents—can expropriate assets for causes other than creating wealth for the shareholders—the owners or principals—for whom they work. Such expropriation is not a form of wealth creation. There is no mutual benefit when assets are expropriated. The shareholders' wealth is transferred to either the corporate manager, or to some persons or entity that the manager favors.

Generally, we can say that when corporate managers use the corporation's resources, they do one of the following:

1. Spend and invest to increase the corporation's value, or
2. Expropriate the corporation's resources, which belong to the shareholders.

Virtually every spending decision can be put into one of these two buckets. Is the manager trying to increase the value of the firm or not? If the manager is spending the corporation's money on things that cannot reasonably be expected to create shareholder value, then the manager is expropriating the corporation's assets. The firm belongs to the shareholders, not to the manager.

Blatant self-dealing, such as setting up a phony business arrangement to funnel cash from the firm to another entity owned by the CEO or a director, is prohibited under the laws of the United States and other industrialized countries. Such things do happen in countries with weak legal protections for shareholders but are uncommon in the United States and other countries with strong shareholder protections.[7]

Softer forms of self-dealing, such as excessive executive compensation, are more difficult to challenge legally. A corporate manager can always argue that an expense is important for the business and worth the cost. It can be argued that a CEO is worth exorbitant pay and will quit otherwise. A case can be made that an elaborate corporate headquarters will attract better employees. Everyone agrees that a CEO's time is very valuable. One could then argue that a CEO needs to fly on a private jet.

In Chapter 2, I explained that the value of a firm is the present value of its cash flow, which is driven by profits. This framework assumes that the firm's cash flow will be used to maximize shareholder value and not expropriated away for other purposes. If that is not the case, then a firm's shares have less value, or even no value, depending on the extent of the expropriation.

We know that extreme amounts of expropriation can destroy a stock market. Investors aren't stupid. If they worry that a corporation's assets are going to be expropriated, then they will be less willing to become shareholders. Multiple studies show that countries with stronger legal protections against expropriation have the following:

- More IPOs
- More publicly traded firms
- Higher market values among the publicly traded firms
- More share issues to fund investment
- Investmentts that are more responsive to growth opportunities[8]

In my corporate finance class, I teach a case study that focuses on expropriation in Russian corporations around the year 2000. The case compares the market capitalization of oil companies, per barrel of oil reserves. At ExxonMobil and British Petroleum, a barrel of oil created about $12 in market capitalization. In contrast, at the Russian oil companies Tatneft and Gazprom, a barrel of oil created only $0.20 in market capitalization.

Why the difference? Corporate governance was terrible in Russia during that time—and still is. Investors knew that most of the profits that Tatneft and Gazprom made would be expropriated by the oligarchs who controlled those companies at that time. In contrast, ExxonMobil and BP had much better governance. Both companies have their shares listed on a U.S. stock exchange and U.S. laws and regulatory agencies make it difficult and costly to expropriate from shareholders.

Institutional Investors and Corporate Governance

Over the past few decades, shareholders increasingly own firms indirectly, through various types of investment funds.[9] I am a shareholder in thousands of companies; however, I don't own a single stock. I own shares in several index funds, which in turn own shares in thousands of different companies around the world.

I do not monitor these companies or keep up with their business decisions. At most, I could name the CEO of a few of them. I have never visited the headquarters of any of them. This is the case for most people who invest in index funds and mutual funds.

Technically, the funds that I invest in own the shares of the various corporations, so the funds are the shareholders of record. This means that when an important matter comes up that requires voting, like an election for the board of directors, the funds do the voting on my behalf. The fund managers are fiduciary agents and are supposed to vote in my best interest.

How should funds approach corporate voting? Thousands of people can invest in a single fund. What do we all have in common? We all prefer more wealth to less. Therefore, funds should vote for directors and policies that will create the maximum value for their investors. This is in line with the fund manager's fiduciary duty, which is to get investors the best possible financial return. In theory, this process should work seamlessly. In reality, we have an additional layer of separation between ownership (shareholders) and control (corporate managers).[10] This creates an additional potential for agency problems and expropriation.

Like corporate managers, investment managers may put their own interests first. They simply may not invest the time and energy needed to be informed voters. They may also pressure corporate managers and directors to use the corporations' resources for social causes that the investment manager favors but that come at the expense of shareholder value. Much of the debate surrounding ESG is about this matter. Some fund managers have been using their voting power to pressure firms to pursue environmental and social causes, many of which are politically divisive. We will explore this issue further in the chapters that follow.

15

LABELS DO NOT CHANGE REALITY

How should we define corporate social responsibility? As discussed in the previous chapter, when corporate managers decide how to spend a corporation's funds they either (a) spend and invest with the intention of increasing shareholder value, or (b) expropriate the firm's resources, which belong to its shareholders.

It is always one of those two actions. What people refer to as "corporate social responsibility" is also one of those two actions. This is true for all the various corporate social responsibility idioms, including environmental, social, and governance (ESG), sustainability, and stakeholder capitalism. Corporate spending is done either (a) with the intention of creating value for the shareholders or (b) as a type of expropriation of the corporation's—that is, the shareholders'—assets. There is no third category.

Anyone can observe a firm's actions and label them "socially responsible" or in the spirit of an ESG rating. Such labels are subjective and depend on who is doing the labeling. *Labels reflect what the labelers like or dislike.* That is all. They have no higher meaning. Labeling an expropriation "socially responsible" does not change the fact that it is an expropriation. If a positive NPV investment lowers a firm's ESG score, it is still a positive NPV investment that created value for the shareholders and society. Attaching a subjective label to something does not change what it is.

Expropriation for a "Social Cause" Is Still Expropriation

Some amount of charitable giving can be good for a corporation's brand. Charitable giving can be categorized as a marketing expense and, like other expenses, it can be a positive NPV investment. It is also true that to go beyond some point of charitable giving creates no additional value for the firm and is then a negative NPV investment. In that case, charitable giving is a de facto donation from the firm's shareholders to the charity.

Consider a CEO of a publicly traded corporation who is very religious. The CEO believes that his religious institution (church, synagogue, or mosque) is important for society. The CEO wants his religion to grow and play a greater role in people's lives. The CEO decides to donate $100 million of the corporation's money to this religious institution. The CEO believes that this donation is the socially responsible thing to do.

Let's assume the CEO does not expect the donation to create value for the corporation. The CEO wants to make the donation because he believes that the religious institution is an important social cause. The CEO does not, however, think that the corporation and its shareholders will get any financial benefit in return, or at least not close to $100 million. This is a negative NPV expenditure. What do we call such a donation?

We call it what it is, expropriation.

The fact that the CEO believes that he gave the corporation's money to an important social cause does not change the fact that he expropriated the shareholders' money. The CEO spent the corporation's money without the intention of creating value for the corporation's shareholders. He did not give away his own money; he gave away the shareholders' money. The CEO decided that the religious institution was worthier of the $100 million than were his company's shareholders, so he transferred the shareholders' money to the religious institution. It's plain vanilla expropriation and nothing more.

Perhaps some of the corporation's shareholders want to donate to this religious institution. Great—they can easily do so. They just go to the institution's website and follow the steps. It takes five minutes. The shareholders don't need the CEO to do it for them. It is also likely that some of the shareholders will disagree with the values and social objectives of the religious institution. Yet their money was donated to it.

One might argue that the shareholders who disagree with the donation can simply sell their shares. That overlooks the fact that the firm is now worth $100 million less, which will be reflected in the price of the shares. Furthermore, investors might now expect more expropriation from the CEO in the future and the share price will reflect that expectation.

Donating to religious institutions is not a common action among publicly traded firms. Corporate social responsibility tends to support progressive causes, rather than more conservative ones like religion, but it is not the nature of the recipient cause that matters. I use this example to make the point that the problem with corporate social responsibility is not that it favors progressive causes, but that it can lead to expropriation from shareholders. I will discuss some specific examples in the next chapter.

Stealing at a Small Business

Consider the previous example in a different setting—a small retail store, with one owner and one employee. The employee has an affinity for various social causes and wants to help. The employee takes money out of the store's cash register and sends it to a nonprofit organization that promotes a social cause that the employee favors. The employee doesn't ask for the owner's permission. How do we describe this?

I don't think there is much disagreement that what the employee did was stealing. We don't justify stealing based on how the proceeds are used.

How is this different from the last example with the CEO? Unlike a CEO of a publicly traded company, a retail store employee is not protected by the business judgment rule, which was discussed in the previous chapter. The CEO and directors of public corporations can get away with making these types of donations. They do so frequently. But ethically and economically, what the CEO did in my fictional example and what the employee at the retail store did are the same thing. They both took cash that belonged to the firms' owners and gave it away.

Shareholder Capitalism by a Different Name

Consider a CEO who offers to buy her employees memberships at a local gym of their choice. She thinks the gym memberships will improve employee health, and that the employees will appreciate the perk. She believes that the benefits to the firm of having happier and healthier employees outweigh the costs of the gym memberships.

The press learns of what the CEO has done and labels her a visionary who is not overly focused on profits but instead considers the firm's employees and other stakeholders. The firm is rewarded with strong ESG and sustainability ratings. Business school professors use the CEO as an example of how great leaders do more than just focus on profits. Case studies are written about the CEO and her firm. MBA students bring her name up in class, signaling to others that they are both virtuous and well informed about current management trends.

The thing is, the CEO did what any profit-seeking CEO would do. She saw an opportunity to increase the value of her firm, and she took it. Why do people need to place additional labels on such things?

For critics of shareholder capitalism, increasing employee perks and compensation always seems to be a good thing, based on the belief that one group, the employees, are worthier of the shareholders' money than the shareholders are. When the critics learn about the gym memberships or some other program that benefits employees, they add a subjective label to it to show that it conforms to their beliefs regarding how the shareholders' money should be spent.

People who don't understand shareholder capitalism are surprised when they learn that it doesn't involve a zero-sum game between shareholders and the other stakeholders. Here are a few corporate actions that can create shareholder value:

- Give employees large raises and generous benefits.
- Enter long-term contracts with suppliers that are profitable to the supplier.
- Lower prices.
- Improve product quality.

All these actions can also reflect terrible business decisions that destroy shareholder value. The corporate manager's job is to evaluate these types of strategies, invest when they create value, and not invest when they destroy value. Conforming to labels that direct the firm's resources toward various social causes is not part of a corporate manager's job description.

Activism as Expropriation

Historically, activist investors target firms that they believe are underperforming financially. Activists buy shares in the firm, and then try to persuade management and the board to pursue a particular strategy, or to operate the firm differently. If the firm's managers are unwilling to go along, the activist may put forth a proposal for the firm's shareholders to vote on. The proposal could be for new directors, or for changes in how the firm is governed or operated. With this type of activism, the activist investor has a financial interest that's aligned with the other shareholders' interests. Activists believe that the firm will be worth more if their proposals are adopted. When activists are successful, all the shareholders gain, not just activists.

Traditional shareholder activism creates shareholder wealth. A large study found that when a known activist investor buys a significant stake in a firm, there is a 5 percent to 10 percent increase in the stock price that does not reverse in the long run.[1] The evidence suggests that activists bring about changes at firms that create lasting value.

A new type of activism—one that pressures firms to pursue ideological causes—has emerged. Unlike traditional investor activism, this new ideological activism does not benefit all shareholders. Instead, these new activists seek to expropriate the firm's resources to support ideological causes that the activists favor. Such activism can destroy shareholder value.

As an example, in 2021, "Follow This," a Dutch nonprofit with the stated goal of reducing carbon dioxide (CO_2) emissions, introduced a shareholder proposal requiring Chevron to reduce its Scope 3 CO_2 emissions.[2] Scope 3 emissions are downstream emissions that are a consequence of a company's activities but occur from entities not owned or controlled by it. A company's customers CO_2 emissions are part of its Scope 3 emissions. Chevron is an oil company. It can reduce its customers' CO_2 emissions only by getting its customers to use less oil. The purpose of this resolution, therefore, was to get Chevron to destroy itself.

In a vote, the majority of Chevron's shareholders approved the proposal. On the surface, this outcome appears puzzling. Aside from an activist promoting an ideological agenda, why would anyone invest in a company and then encourage it to destroy itself?

The proposal passed because most of Chevron's shareholders own its stock indirectly, through investment funds. As discussed in the previous chapter, the fund managers, not the investors in their funds, vote on these proposals. The world's three largest fund managers, BlackRock, State Street, and Vanguard, all voted to support the proposal.[3]

The persons managing BlackRock, State Street, and Vanguard have an ideological agenda. All three firms have publicly supported the idea of pressuring corporations to reduce CO_2 emissions, although Vanguard has since backed away from this.[4] In the case of Chevron, these fund managers decided to put that ideological agenda ahead of their fiduciary duty, which is to maximize their investors' financial returns. Any reduction to Chevron's value resulting from this resolution is an expropriation from Chevron's shareholders to the ideological cause of not using fossil fuels. Despite this resolution, in all likelihood, we will continue to use fossil fuels. To the extent that this proposal is binding, the oil will be produced by other firms.

The activists and fund companies that attacked Chevron claim to represent society. But society elected the government that regulates Chevron. The U.S. Environmental Protection Agency currently has about 170,000 outstanding regulations, each containing multiple rules, that Chevron has to obey.[5] Reducing its customers' CO_2 emissions is not one of them. The activists would like to have this regulation, though. They can't get it via elections, so they try a different tactic and claim to be acting on behalf of society. In reality, the activists are pursuing an ideological agenda that the majority of voters does not want.

Socially Responsible Investing versus Socially Responsible Activism

There is an important difference between socially responsible *investing* and socially responsible *activism*. An investor who thinks oil is bad for the world, and thus decides not to invest in Chevron, is not harming anyone else. If you don't like a business, then don't invest in it. Any potential investor or stakeholder who does not approve of a company or its products should be free to choose not to transact with that company. Such freedom of choice is the essence of capitalism.

There are "socially responsible" funds that investors can choose to invest in. Most socially responsible funds use social and environmental criteria to screen out companies, but they don't engage in activism. Such funds aren't in conflict with shareholder capitalism. As an example, BlackRock offers a fund, iShares ESG Aware, that screens out companies involved in "civilian firearms, controversial weapons, tobacco, thermal coal, and oil sands."[6] If investors want this type of fund, and BlackRock can profitably offer one, then doing so is perfectly consistent with capitalism. By the same token, there are funds that focus on fossil fuel investments, such as the Vanguard Energy ETF, or State Street's SPDR S&P Oil & Gas Exploration ETF. Investors might choose these funds if they believe that fossil fuel companies are undervalued. Other investors may believe that it's socially responsible to ensure that humanity has access to abundant, inexpensive fossil fuels. Has any modern society escaped poverty without using fossil fuels?

The problems with socially responsible funds are with the labeling and clarity about expected investment performance. The label of "socially responsible" or "environmentally conscious" is completely subjective. Different persons can have different opinions on what constitutes sound social and environmental policies. A more accurate label for "socially responsible investing" would be "ideology-driven investing" or "cause-driven investing."

If a fund screens out companies on the basis of social and environmental criteria, it reduces its universe of investment opportunities. Compared with a fund that does not have such constraints, the socially responsible fund has fewer investment choices.

The socially responsible fund's performance should therefore be worse than that of funds that don't impose such constraints. As Cliff Asness, owner of the large asset management firm AQR, which offers multiple ESG funds, explains:

> Put simply, if two investors approach an asset manager, one who says "just maximize my return for the risk taken" and the other who says "do that but subject to the following constraints," it is simply false and irresponsible for the asset manager to assert that the second investor should expect to do as well as the first, except in the case where those constraints are non-binding (and therefore not relevant).[7]

In some periods, socially responsible funds may outperform other funds. For example, there will be periods when oil stocks happen to perform poorly. During such times, funds that screen out oil stocks will do relatively well. But over a long enough period of time, funds that face a limited investment universe will perform worse relative to funds that do not.

Shareholder Capitalism and the ESG Moniker

Some of the components of corporate social responsibility metrics, such as ESG scores, may reward firms with higher scores for actions that are consistent with shareholder capitalism. For example, firms may receive lower ESG scores if they are fined for violating environmental regulations or employee safety regulations. This is consistent with shareholder capitalism, under which firms are supposed to follow regulations. ESG proponents point out that following environmental and other regulations can increase shareholder value, because doing so is good for the firm's brand and reduces the chance of costly lawsuits. True, but there is nothing new here; people understood the importance of reputation and avoiding costly lawsuits long before ESG came on the scene.

A 2022 study by Massachusetts Institute of Technology (MIT) researchers examines ESG scores from six major rating agencies.[8] It reports that among the six agencies, there are 709 metrics used to create the ESG scores. The researchers explain that the 709 metrics are quite diverse and can be grouped into 64 categories. It would not be surprising to learn that some of the 709 indicators encourage maximizing shareholder value, while others do not. ESG proponents argue that because *some* of the indicators are correlated with shareholder value, it is good for shareholders if firms strive for better ESG ratings. The problem with this logic is that some of the ESG indicators encourage activities that reduce shareholder value. If it were the case that pursuing ESG *always* results in higher shareholder value, then ESG would be shareholder capitalism by another name.

In general, we can say the following:

- If an action increases shareholder value but reduces the ESG score, the firm *should* take the action.
- If an action reduces shareholder value but increases the ESG score, the firm *should not* take the action.

The ESG score is not an economic outcome like shareholder value. Shareholder value reflects the *creation of wealth* resulting from mutually beneficial trading. ESG is a metric that someone made up; anyone can issue an ESG score. You or I could issue our own ESG rating and it would be no less legitimate than the ones currently being issued.

The MIT study also finds that there is substantial disagreement among the six ESG scores. It examines a large sample of firms that were assigned scores by each of the six ratings agencies. It reports that the correlations, which can range from -1 (complete disagreement) to 1 (complete agreement) among the six ESG scores range from 0.31 to 0.78. Describing this result in a *Wall Street Journal* article, one of the study's authors wrote, "In other words, the six never all agreed on a company's ESG rating, and in most cases there was little agreement among them."[9] Even the number of indicators used to create the ratings varied greatly, ranging from 38 for one rating agency to 282 for another.

The disagreement among ESG scores and scoring methodologies is not surprising; what constitutes sound environmental and social policies is subjective. We could average the six ESG scores to come up with a single rating, but averaging six subjective variables does not create an objective one.

16

CORPORATE SOCIAL RESPONSIBILITY OR CORPORATE POLITICAL ACTIVISM?

If a policy or corporate action is clearly in society's best interest, then it should not be controversial. It should be easy to convince most people that the policy or action is a good idea. Yet that is not the case with corporate social responsibility.

The various corporate social responsibility frameworks that have been put forth over the years argue that firms have a greater responsibility to society, beyond just making profits, that is not addressed by regulations. OK, but then who gets to decide what that responsibility is? People can disagree on what constitutes a socially responsible action. So, who gets to decide what is socially responsible? It's not the government or anyone who was elected to anything. Therein lies the problem with corporate social responsibility. It is entirely subjective. What then matters is *who gets to decide* what is socially responsible and what is not.

How this works in practice is that an unelected party decides that it speaks for society. It observes how firms operate and labels firms and their activities as either good or bad for society. Which corporate activities are good, and which are bad, is a distinction based on the ideological beliefs of the person or persons doing the labeling. Currently, those doing the labeling tend to favor progressive causes. Conservatives can also label things, but in practice, the various social responsibility frameworks tend to encourage policies favored by progressives.[1] What we refer to as corporate social responsibility is better described as corporate political activism.

Taking Responsibility or Promoting Ideological Causes?

Here are some recent examples of social responsibility initiatives at public corporations. See if you can identify a common pattern. I am not arguing that these initiatives are good or bad. My point is that they have a common ideological bent.

- In response to the Supreme Court overturning *Roe v. Wade*, several companies, including Amazon, Bank of America, Citigroup, Goldman Sachs, Hewlett Packard, JPMorgan Chase, Microsoft, Walt Disney, and Yahoo, announced that they will provide abortion travel coverage as a benefit to employees living in states where abortion is restricted.[2]
- Coca-Cola, Microsoft, Capital One, Pfizer, Citigroup, Amazon, and Starbucks all donated to the Human Rights Campaign, the largest LGBTQ advocacy lobbying group in the United States.[3] It endorses political candidates, almost always Democrats.[4]
- In 2021, 200 corporations signed a letter criticizing voter ID laws. The signatories included PayPal, United Airlines, and Uber, all of which require an ID to use their services.[5]
- United Airlines announced that it planned to fill half of its 5,000 pilot positions opening up over the next decade with women or "people of color."[6]
- Amazon, Microsoft, Coca-Cola, and Airbnb have donated to Black Lives Matter, which raised $90 million in 2020.

The group, whose founders are self-proclaimed "trained Marxists,"[7] has advocated for controversial policies such as "defunding the police."[8]

Would the typical Republican support any of these initiatives? Plenty of Democrats might have reservations about some of these efforts. Even shareholders who agree with these causes may not want their money spent this way. If shareholders want to contribute to these causes, they can easily do so on their own. If someone wants to donate to the Human Rights Campaign or Black Lives Matter, they can simply go to the organization's website and make a donation.

In a functioning democracy, some people will support progressive social causes, others will support conservative ones, and others will not care so much and support none. That is as it should be. People should be able to speak freely and spend their *own money* as they see fit. The problem here is that managers of public corporations are using *the corporation's assets* to promote ideological causes. When a corporate manager uses the corporation's—that is, the shareholder's—assets to fund a social cause that she favors, it is a type of expropriation.

Expropriation to fund social causes can be worse than traditional expropriation, in which there is only a wealth transfer from the shareholders to the corporate manager or controlling shareholder. With social responsibility expropriation, there is not only a loss of shareholder wealth but also the funding of ideological agendas that many of the shareholders oppose.

Financial Institutions and CO_2 Emissions

There is currently much disagreement over whether and how to regulate CO_2 emissions. It is a highly partisan issue. Progressives tend to favor policies limiting the use of fossil fuels, whereas most

Republicans and some moderate Democrats oppose them.[9] There is currently no U.S. regulation that explicitly limits CO_2 emissions. We could have such a regulation, but we do not. So, as it stands, you are free to produce as much CO_2 emissions as you like.

Several fund managers and publicly traded banks have taken it upon themselves to act as de facto regulators on this matter. They have joined consortiums with the stated goal of eliminating CO_2 emissions by 2050. One such consortium is the Net Zero Asset Managers initiative. Its members include 301 fund managers with more than $59 trillion in assets under management.[10] The United Nations (UN) played a role in its founding. Here is how the Net Zero Asset Managers initiative describes its purpose:

> The Net Zero Asset Managers initiative is an international group of asset managers committed to supporting the goal of net zero greenhouse gas emissions by 2050 or sooner, in line with global efforts to limit warming to 1.5 degrees Celsius; and to supporting investing aligned with net zero emissions by 2050 or sooner.[11]

Climate Action 100+ is a similar fund manager consortium. Its members include more than 700 investors with $68 trillion in assets.[12] It "engages" with 166 companies that are major emitters of CO_2 emissions. Climate Action 100+ asks this of its members:

> To mitigate their exposure and secure ongoing sustainable returns for their beneficiaries, investors must ensure the businesses they own have strategies that accelerate the transition to net-zero emissions by 2050, or sooner and align with the goal of the Paris Agreement, of limiting average global temperature rise to well below two degrees Celsius above pre-industrial levels, and pursuing efforts even further to limit the temperature increase to 1.5 degrees Celsius.[13]

Both consortiums and their members are clearly engaging in political activism. The consortiums are trying to enforce a policy that their members and the UN favor, in place of what people have voted for. The Paris Agreement is not a law or regulation that is binding on any American firm. Under the Biden administration, the United States is a signatory to the Paris Agreement, but the executive branch alone cannot enact laws or enter into treaties. The Paris Agreement was never ratified by the Senate. It governs nothing in the United States. Politicians could enact legislation consistent with the Paris Agreement's aims but have chosen not to. The same is true for virtually all countries that are signatories to the Paris Agreement.[14]

There is evidence that these fund manager alliances have been effective. A 2022 survey of oil and gas firms by the Federal Reserve Bank of Dallas asked the primary reason for low investment among publicly traded oil producers, despite high oil prices. Fifty-nine percent of the respondents named pressure from investors as the primary reason.[15] A respondent to a similar Dallas Fed survey from 2021 wrote that it had relationships with approximately 400 institutional investors, but that only one was willing to provide capital for oil and gas investment.[16]

The Net-Zero Banking Alliance is another UN initiative. Its goal is to reach net zero CO_2 emissions by 2050.[17] The alliance has 122 member banks from 41 countries that together account for 40 percent of global banking assets. The commitment statement, which each bank signs when it joins the consortium, states the following:

> Transition all operational and attributable GHG [greenhouse gas] emissions from our lending and investment portfolios to align with pathways to net-zero by mid-century, or sooner, including CO_2 emissions reaching net-zero at the latest by 2050, consistent with a maximum temperature rise of 1.5°C above pre-industrial levels by 2100. . . . GHG emissions here refer to banks' Scope 1, 2 and 3 emissions. Banks' Scope 3 emissions should include their clients' Scope 1 and 2 and Scope 3 emissions, where significant, and where data allow.[18]

This statement basically says that banks should not lend to fossil fuel companies. As discussed in Chapter 14, Scope 3 CO_2 emissions include customers' CO_2 emissions. So, this commitment says that banks not only have to get their own greenhouse gas emissions down to zero, but also their clients' emissions and their clients' customers' emissions. If an oil company is a bank's client, the bank's Scope 3 emissions reflect customers using that oil company's product. For an oil company to get its Scope 3 CO_2 emissions down to zero, it needs to stop selling oil.

There is nothing wrong with privately held banks entering such consortiums, at least from the perspective of shareholder capitalism, but with publicly traded banks it is a different story. Publicly traded banks belong to their shareholders, not to their executives. When these banks skip profitable lending opportunities to instead pursue political agendas—such as on climate change—they reduce shareholder value.

Investigations and Legal Actions by Republican Attorneys General

Recent legal actions and investigations by Republican state attorneys general (AGs) and other Republican politicians further indicate that much of what is called corporate social responsibility is better described as corporate political activism. In total, 27 states have taken legal actions or filed complaints to limit ESG investing.[19] These actions don't mean that the social and environmental causes associated with ESG are good or bad causes, but they do show that the causes are highly partisan. If ESG focused on objective metrics, like profits, then the majority of states in the nation would not be taking legal action to limit it.

The Republican AGs' legal complaint is that when their state pension funds invest with fund managers, the managers have a fiduciary duty to get the pensioners the highest possible financial return. Yet some fund managers have been encouraging the firms that they invest in to pursue various social causes, which may come at the expense of financial returns. The AGs first set their sights on BlackRock and its CEO Larry Fink, who is one of corporate social responsibility's greatest promoters. BlackRock is the world's largest fund manager, so it can influence the companies in which it invests. As explained in Chapter 14, the fund managers are the shareholders of record and therefore vote on corporate policies and in elections for directors. BlackRock is also a signatory to the two asset manager consortiums discussed previously. A letter from 19 Republican AGs to Fink stated the following:

> Based on the facts currently available to us, BlackRock appears to use the hard-earned money of our states' citizens to circumvent the best possible return on investment, as well as their vote. BlackRock's past public commitments indicate that it has used citizens' assets to pressure companies to comply with international agreements such as the Paris Agreement that force the phase-out of fossil fuels, increase energy prices, drive inflation, and weaken the national security of the United States. These agreements have never been ratified by the United States Senate. The Senators elected by the citizens of this country determine which international agreements have the force of law, not BlackRock.[20]

In March 2023, 21 Republican AGs wrote a similar open letter to the 53 largest U.S. asset managers. The letter expressed concern that the asset managers were using their voting power to pressure firms to comply with various ESG goals, including the goal of zero CO_2 emissions by 2050. Other issues discussed in the letter include shareholder proposals concerned with race and gender quotas, proposals that would effectively require firms to issue reports explaining political donations to Republicans but not to Democrats, and proposals requiring firms to issue reports on how operating in states that passed laws limiting abortion create business risk to the firm.

The Republican AGs also initiated an investigation into Morningstar, a company that rates mutual fund performance, and its subsidiary, Sustainalytics, which issues ESG ratings.[21] Sustainalytics' ratings are important, because fund managers with an ESG focus may make investment decisions based on these ratings. The AGs argue that Sustainalytics' ESG ratings have an anti-Israel bias, as companies that do business with Israel received lower ESG ratings. My point here is not to take a side on policies concerning Israel, which can evoke strong disagreement, but that such policies are inherently political.

With shareholder capitalism, we don't have any of these controversies. The fund manager's job is to serve as a fiduciary for its investors. The funds' investors benefit from increases in firm value. The fund manager, therefore, votes for policies that he believes will increase shareholder value. You and the people managing your funds can be polar opposites politically, but the fund manager still does the job you hired him to do. In this sense, fund managers are no different from accountants or dentists. They simply do the job that they are tasked with. Investors don't have to worry that their savings are being used to promote social and environmental causes that they disagree with and may have even voted against.

What's Wrong with Corporate Political Activism?

Imagine that you and I own a corporation together. I own 55 percent of the corporation, while you own the other 45 percent. I, therefore, control how the corporation is operated. We get along well and usually agree on how to run the business, and the business is successful and growing. On matters of politics, though, we are polar opposites.

I decide that it's not enough for our corporation to be profitable and that it also needs to be socially responsible. I am the controlling shareholder, so I get to define what socially responsible means. I donate some of our corporation's profits to ideological causes that I favor. I draft up corporate statements on partisan issues. I ask guest speakers who share my views to visit our company and speak about partisan issues. These actions not only use corporate assets that belong to you, they also promote ideological causes that contradict your beliefs and values. After all of this, would you want to keep partnering with me? Would you invest in a second business with me?

It's no different with a publicly traded corporation. When corporate executives use the assets of a corporation to advance ideological causes, they expropriate from the shareholders and cause additional injury to shareholders that disagree with the ideology. If corporate political activism becomes the norm, it could mean fewer people investing in publicly traded companies. As discussed in chapter 14, many studies show that countries with more corporate expropriation have thinner stock markets.

Corporate partisanship is harmful to our democracy, in which the outcomes of elections are supposed to determine our environmental and social policies. With corporate partisanship, people use corporations to promote the environmental and social causes that they favor but could not get implemented through the electoral process. We then have a small, unelected group deciding what is good or bad for society. Such actions make Americans more fractured along partisan lines. In contrast, shareholder capitalism puts everyone on the same page. All shareholders benefit when the corporation is successful.

Shareholders are a diverse group politically. According to a 2022 Gallup poll, 65 percent of Republicans, 61 percent of Democrats, and 53 percent of independents own equities.[22] If we play by the rules of shareholder capitalism, such differences are irrelevant. The shareholders can peacefully coexist. The goal of the firm is to maximize shareholder value; all shareholders gain when the firm performs well. Progressive shareholders and conservative shareholders—and even those who don't pay attention to politics—can all agree that a +10 percent return on investment is better than a −10 percent return.

17

DOES CORPORATE SOCIAL RESPONSIBILITY
REMEDY REGULATORY FAILURES?

At the beginning of this book, I wrote about the earliest evidence of trade, which dates back more than 300,000 years. The evidence includes tools made from black obsidian, a volcanic rock that can be easily shaped into sharp objects. Also found at the excavation site is the earliest evidence of industrial waste. Creating the tools required chipping away at the obsidian until it was the desired shape and sharpness. The toolmakers left behind 46,000 obsidian chips that were discovered by archaeologists.[1] We humans apparently have a long history of not cleaning up after ourselves. With this in mind, let's try to make a case for corporate social responsibility.

Corporate social responsibility could correct negative externalities left unaddressed by regulation. A negative externality occurs when two parties trade and a third party that did not benefit from the trade bears some cost created by the trade. Pollution is a classic example. People who live close to a polluting firm may suffer the costs of the pollution even though they do not receive any benefits from trading with the firm.

The shareholders of the polluting firm may also suffer from the pollution or from knowing that the pollution harms others. Economists Oliver Hart, winner of the Nobel Prize in Economics, and Luigi Zingales point out that the cost of some externalities *to the shareholders* could be greater than the shareholder value created by the externality.[2] So, although reducing pollution is costly and reduces profits and shareholder value, the harm of the pollution to the shareholders may be greater than the loss in shareholder value. Thus, *shareholder welfare* is higher if the firm reduces pollution, even though *shareholder value* is lower. This is a clever argument. It works in theory. But does it help explain the real world?

If there is widespread agreement that an externality creates significant harm, then why don't we pass a regulation that limits it? I agree with Hart and Zingales that there are externalities that shareholders favor reducing even if doing so reduces their wealth. No one wants toxic waste dumped into our rivers and lakes, even if it's an inexpensive way to dispose of it. Yet such blatant externalities are almost surely going to be regulated. If an externality is not regulated, it is probably because most of society feels that the regulation is not warranted.

Corporate social responsibility is also a poor means by which to address important externalities and other social problems. There are more than 33 million businesses registered in the United States that are privately owned and therefore less affected by ESG ratings and corporate social responsibility campaigns.[3] The 4,200 U.S. publicly traded corporations are on average much larger than most private businesses, but, in aggregate, private businesses are economically important.[4]

Is It Difficult to Implement New Regulations?

It is not difficult to implement new regulations. As discussed in Chapter 1, there are so many regulations covering so many areas of the economy that the total number of rules and restrictions that a business faces is unknowable. No one could read the entire Code of Federal Regulations. To get an estimate for a particular business, one needs to write a computer program that can search through the federal code using various keywords. The *New York Times* reported in 2017 on how many federal rules and restrictions an apple orchard has to deal with.[5] It estimated that there are about 12,000 federal rules that apple orchards must comply with. Most of those rules apply to other businesses besides orchards. There are 5,000 rules written specifically for orchards. These rules stem from 17 regulations, so each regulation has on average 294 rules. If we extrapolate that to the entire economy, then there are potentially hundreds of millions of rules and restrictions contained in the 1,091,796 federal regulations that were on the books at the end of 2022.

State and local governments have their own regulations as well. The average U.S. state has 138,841 regulations.[6] The state with the greatest number of regulations is California with 403,774.[7] The state with the least number of regulations is Idaho, with 36,612.[8] Does California have too many, or does Idaho have too few? I'll let you decide.

The most prolific federal agency at issuing regulations is the Environmental Protection Agency (EPA). The EPA currently has about 170,000 regulations on the books, more than any other federal agency.[9] The EPA was founded in 1970 by President Richard Nixon. Since then, it has averaged more than 3,000 new regulations per year.

Democrats tend to want stricter environmental regulations than Republicans. In President Obama's first term, the EPA enacted 16,583 new regulations.[10] Some people thought that that was too many, and others thought it did not go far enough. President Trump rescinded 100 of the EPA's costlier rules.[11] That action upset some people and made others happy. President Biden has worked to reverse this and add more.[12] This is how things are supposed to work in a democracy. Elections have consequences and lead to regulations that reflect the majority's preference.

The argument that we cannot regulate externalities when there is widespread agreement that the externality is significantly harmful does not hold water. If anything, it's too easy for agencies to implement new regulations, and regulators often fail to fully consider the costs of the regulations that they impose. If an environmental externality is not regulated, it's likely that most people don't want it to be, rather than some invisible force preventing regulators from enacting the people's will.

Does Corporate Social Responsibility Correct the Negative Externalities Caused by CO_2 Emissions?

The previous chapter discussed the fund manager and banker consortiums that were convened to get the world to net zero CO_2 emissions by the year 2050. Could that movement be described as working to implement a de facto regulation that most Americans want as government policy but for some reason cannot have?

An argument that I often hear in academic circles goes as follows. CO_2 emissions contribute to global warming, which is costly, but firms don't directly bear these costs because the emissions are not priced. The costs to society of CO_2 emissions do not make firms' current profits lower. Thus, firms use more fossil fuels than they would if the costs of global warming were accurately reflected in the price of fossil fuels. Can this framework explain the net zero campaign? Is it just a means for correcting a market failure?

The problem with this argument is that the net zero campaign doesn't change the price of fossil fuels to reflect the costs of global warming. Rather, it aims to *eliminate* the use of fossil fuels entirely. Fossil fuels may create negative externalities, but they also have enormous benefits—namely, affordable and reliable energy. Therefore, the cost of eliminating fossil fuels is likely to be very high, much higher than what most people are willing to pay.

Most people respond "Yes" if simply asked, "Do you want corporations to generate fewer CO_2 emissions?" Yet most people respond "No" if asked, "Are you willing to pay the actual cost of the lowering corporate emissions?" A 2018 poll by AP-NORC Center for Public Affairs Research found that 68 percent of Americans are unwilling to pay an extra $10 per month in electric bills to combat global warming.[13] Similarly, a 2019 Kaiser Family Foundation poll found that 71 percent were unwilling to pay a $10 per month tax to combat global warming and 74 percent were opposed to a $0.25 per gallon gasoline tax.[14]

How much would getting to net zero emissions by 2050 cost? It is impossible to know for sure, but we can examine some estimates. A 2021 study published in the journal *Nature Climate Change* estimates that a 95 percent reduction in emissions by 2050 could cost the United States as much as 11.9 percent of GDP, or $11,300 *per person,* annually.[15] The same study shows that a more modest reduction of 60 percent by 2050 would still cost $1,913 per person annually. New Zealand recently committed to net zero greenhouse gas emissions by 2050. An independent consulting firm hired by the New Zealand government estimates, in a report that wasn't highly publicized, that by 2050 net zero could cost New Zealand between 10 percent and 21 percent of its GDP.[16]

If the United States alone were to achieve the goal of zero CO_2 emissions by 2050, it would matter little for global temperatures. The UN's climate model shows that if the United States went to zero emissions immediately, it would affect global temperatures by only 0.3 degrees Fahrenheit by 2100.[17] The reason is that the United States is expected to become less important with respect to global greenhouse gas emissions over time, with India, China, and Africa expected to make up an increasingly larger share.

The Costs of Climate Change

Maybe the fund managers and bankers are right and the rest of us are wrong. The net zero 2050 campaign may be expensive, but perhaps the costs of global warming are even greater. If so, then net zero is the better strategy for us to follow. So how expensive are the effects of global warming expected to be? No one really knows, and anyone can create a model that makes a forecast. With this in mind, let's look at estimates from sources that should be relatively well informed on the topic.

The United Nations' 2018 climate panel report estimates that if we do nothing to reduce CO_2 emissions, and continue as we have been, the costs of global warming will be 2.6 percent of global GDP by 2100.[18] How big a deal is this? To put it in perspective, the global economy grows on average by 2 percent or 3 percent per year. If global warming costs us 2.6 percent of global GDP, it is equivalent to about one year of global GDP growth. People living in 2100 would need one year of growth to catch up to where they would have been if there were no global warming. For a person in 2100, it's hardly noticeable and certainly not the apocalypse.

Perhaps the UN's estimate is way off? A recent study on this topic models 800 plausible specifications of the temperature–GDP relationship. It estimates that the annual cost of unmitigated climate change will be between 1 percent and 3 percent of global GDP by 2100, right around the UN's estimate of 2.6 percent.[19]

Another factor to consider is that people living in 2100 will in all likelihood be much richer than we are today, regardless of how the climate evolves. If GDP per capita grows at 2 percent per year from now until 2100, global gross domestic product per capita will be 450 percent greater in 2100 than today. This means that the average person in 2100 would be 450 percent richer than the average person today. If GDP per capita grows at 3 percent per year, the average person in 2100 will be 945 percent richer. Even if the cost of climate change by 2100 were double or triple the UN estimate of 2.6 percent of GDP, the average person living then will still have much higher living standards than we do today.

The costs and benefits of various strategies to combat climate change can also be estimated with the DICE model (for Dynamic Integrated Model of Climate and the Economy), which was created by William Nordhaus, winner of the Nobel Prize in Economics in 2018 for his work on climate change and economic policy.[20] The DICE model allows the user to enter in various scenarios and then estimates both the costs of climate change and the cost of reducing CO_2 emissions in an effort to mitigate climate change. The DICE model assumes that the costs of climate change in 2100 will be 46 percent higher than the UN's estimate.[21]

Bjorn Lomborg, director of the Copenhagen Consensus Center, used the DICE model to create the chart displayed in Figure 17.1.[22] Lomborg's analysis shows that although global warming is likely to have significant costs, so does replacing fossil fuels with more expensive sources of energy. We need to consider both costs when evaluating our options.

Figure 17.1: How to find the smartest climate policy, temperature in 2100 from different climate policies, present-day value of costs of climate and climate policy, in trillions of 2010 dollars

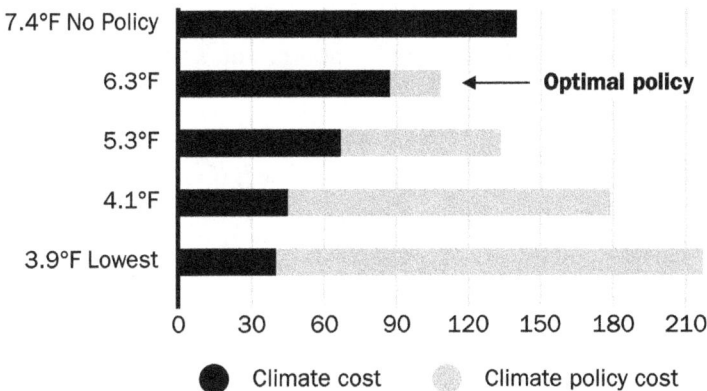

Source: Bjorn Lomborg, "A Reasonable Alternative to COP26 and Preaching Climate Doom," *Wall Street Journal,* November 10, 2021.

The chart shows that if society continues as it has, and does nothing to reduce CO_2 emissions, the average temperature is expected to increase by 7.4°F by 2100, compared with 1900. The total cost of following this policy is about $140 trillion. It is not the best path but also not the worst. The most expensive path is the one with the greatest reduction in fossil fuels. It leads to the smallest increase in temperature, 3.9°F, and gets us closest to net zero emissions by the 2050 marker but comes with total costs of $215 trillion.

The optimal path with the lowest costs leads to an average temperature increase of 6.3°F and has total costs of about $115 trillion. This path includes a carbon tax, which increases the price of fossil fuels to reflect the cost of global warming. The policy begins with a relatively small tax and increases slowly over time, as we figure out better ways to generate energy that is free of CO_2 emissions.

The DICE model assumes that the *entire world* follows the same policy. If the United States and Europe aim for net zero by 2050, but China, India, and the rest of the developing world continue to grow and rely on fossil fuels, then we still end up with a temperature increase that is close to 7.4°F. Americans and Europeans will have then paid a very high cost but received no benefits. Our descendants will be poorer and still face the challenges of higher temperatures.

I am not writing all of this to advocate one path over the other. As far as shareholder capitalism is concerned, if net zero emissions by 2050 becomes government policy, then firms need to comply with it. My point is that net zero isn't an example of corporate social responsibility giving us a regulation that we want but cannot have because of political dysfunction. Nor is it an example of wise people at the United Nations and financial institutions saving us from ourselves. Rather, the net zero 2050 consortiums are best described as unelected people attempting to implement public policies that have been rejected through the democratic political process.

Why Stop at Climate Change?

Should we expect the consortiums to go away if the issues with CO_2 emissions get resolved? There's no reason to think that will be the case. If the consortiums can successfully act as de facto regulators for fossil fuels, then they could do so for other social and environmental issues as well. Thus, rather than disappear, the consortiums are likely to move on to the next social cause. If a business provides goods or services that are contrary to that cause, the consortiums can starve it of capital. Perhaps an entrepreneur or CEO voices a political view contrary to the agenda that the consortiums are trying to promote. The CEO's company could be blacklisted and starved of capital.

Corporate social responsibility could fundamentally change the financial industry's role in the economy and society. If a firm has valuable growth opportunities but is not deemed to be socially responsible by the United Nations and the finance industry, it may not get access to capital. Yet a firm has valuable growth opportunities because it can create goods and services that are valued by society. If corporate social responsibility consortiums prevent such firms from raising capital, then the consortiums are effectively overruling society. Do we want financiers—or anyone—to have this power?

The End of One Person, One Vote?

Democracy is by no means perfect, but if we are going to make a major decision like quitting fossil fuels by 2050, which affects everyone, it is better to do it through a democratic process, where everyone gets the chance to vote. Each citizen does not have an equal voice in corporate voting, as we do in political voting.[23] While our system of government is based on one person, one vote, corporate voting is based on the ownership of shares. People who do not own shares do not get to vote on corporate policies and in directors' elections. Forty-two percent of Americans are not shareholders, but they deserve to have a say in how society is regulated and what sources of energy they are allowed to use.[24]

To make matters worse, as discussed in Chapter 14, it is primarily fund managers, not individual investors, who vote in corporate elections and on corporate proposals. We would not let Larry Fink vote on behalf of millions of people in a government election, as BlackRock does at shareholder meetings. That is why the fund manager consortiums can have so much power; a small number of fund managers get to vote on behalf of millions of shareholders. This arrangement works well if the fund managers are simply trying to get their investors the best possible financial returns, which is their fiduciary duty. But on public policy matters, the fund managers' votes will reflect the managers' preferences, which will be different from the preferences of many of the shareholders, most of whom have no idea that a vote is taking place or how corporate voting works, for that matter.

For all these reasons, representative democracy is the more sensible approach toward regulation. Government regulation is far from perfect. There is much research showing that too often regulation creates significant costs with little benefit.[25] But at least with government everyone gets a chance to vote and have a say in how society is regulated.

18

SUSTAINABILITY THEN AND NOW

Short of thermonuclear war itself, population growth is the gravest issue the world faces over the decades immediately ahead. . . . Indeed, in many ways rampant population growth is an even more dangerous and subtle threat to the world than thermonuclear war, for it is intrinsically less subject to rational safeguards, and less amenable to organized control.[1]

—*Robert McNamara*

One of the most popular terms in the corporate social responsibility lingo is sustainability. What constitutes a sustainable business? As with the other social responsibility labels, the answer depends on who is doing the labeling. The more relevant question is: Who gets to decide what is sustainable? The sustainability label often refers to environmental issues, such as reducing carbon emissions but can include other social causes, such as workforce diversity.

Sustainability in business today is reminiscent of the dot-com bubble around the year 2000. One study found that during that time, if a firm added ".com" to its name, it had a significant increase in stock price.[2] It did not matter what business the firm was in. Simply changing the name to suggest an online presence added millions of dollars in market capitalization. If you were to visit a business school during that time, MBA students would be eager to tell you how their work experience involved the internet. Many were hoping to get internet-related jobs, preferably at startups. Various business school faculty, who several years earlier had no teaching experience or research related to the internet, were now experts in all things online and how it was changing business. Consultants suddenly had all sorts of expertise in helping firms transition to the new dot-com world. And so too it is today with sustainability.

Today's sustainability ideology grew out of the previous version, which claimed that both population growth and economic growth were unsustainable. Past sustainability experts had, by their own lights, figured out how many people could sustainably live on the planet and how much each person could sustainably consume. This view was popularized during the 1960s and 1970s. It was promoted by academics at elite universities, including Berkeley, MIT, and Stanford, and by global organizations, including the World Economic Forum, World Bank, and United Nations—the same institutions that are at the forefront of promoting today's sustainability ideology.

This chapter focuses on two points regarding sustainability as it pertains to business and economics.

- The definition of sustainability in the context of economics has changed significantly over the past half century. It has changed because the claims of the original sustainability ideology were proven wrong. Yet the same institutions that promoted the original sustainability ideology, including those just mentioned, are taking the lead in promoting the new one.

- There is no such thing as a sustainable business in a functioning market economy. No business or business practice is sustainable in a developed economy that is characterized by creative destruction and economic growth.

The Original Sustainability Ideology

The core argument of the original sustainability ideology is that the world has too many people. This claim was popularized back in the 1960s, when the world's population was half of what it is today. The experts claimed that the planet's resources were being rapidly depleted. A new global government was needed to end both population growth and economic growth. Wealth needed to move from rich nations to poor nations, so that there would be global equality across all countries. The sustainability experts were effectively advocating for economic central planning and strict controls on human reproduction—the same kind of policies that were implemented in Mao's China during that time.

The original sustainability ideology had severe effects on humanity. Millions were sterilized in Mexico, Bolivia, Peru, Indonesia, and Bangladesh.[3] In Egypt, Tunisia, Pakistan, South Korea, and Taiwan, health workers' salaries depended on the number of intrauterine devices, or IUDs, they inserted in women.[4] India began a sterilization campaign in the 1970s. In several Indian states, sterilization was required in order for men and women to obtain water, electricity, ration cards, medical care, and pay raises.[5] India sterilized 6.2 million poor men in 1975 alone.[6] India's efforts were encouraged by millions of dollars in loans from the World Bank and the UN population fund.[7] In 1976, then-World Bank president Robert McNamara stated that, "At long last . . . India is moving to effectively address its population problem." In total, the World Bank loaned India $66 million for "population control."[8]

China instituted its one-child policy in 1979 and ended it in 2015. Its enforcement included both millions of forced sterilizations and perhaps as many as 100 million forced abortions.[9] Local program administrators were given bonuses based on the number of abortions and sterilizations in their regions.[10]

In some regions, women who became pregnant with a second child were given the choice of job loss or an abortion. If born, the second child would not be a citizen and thus not allowed to attend school or count toward a family's food ration.[11] China's one-child policy was inspired by a 1972 book, *The Limits to Growth*, which was promoted by the World Economic Forum at its 1973 Davos meeting.[12]

In 1983, the United Nations Population Fund began to issue the "Population Award" to "an individual or individuals, or to an institution or institutions . . . for the most outstanding contribution to the awareness of population questions or to their solutions."[13] The first winners were Indian Prime Minister Indira Gandhi, who oversaw India's sterilization campaign, and Chinese Health Minister Qian Xinzhong, who oversaw China's one-child policy.[14] The UN had been promoting population control polices long before this. The UN Population Commission was established in 1946. One of the Population Commission's founding mandates was to advise the UN Economic and Social Council on "Policies designed to influence the size and structure of populations and the changes therein."[15]

In 1966, the United States set up an Office of Population within the U.S. Agency for International Development (USAID).[16] Its first director, Dr. Reimert Ravenholt, stated that one-quarter of the world's fertile women had to be sterilized for the United States to meet its goals for population control.[17] U.S. foreign aid to poor countries was tied to population control.[18] The World Bank tied population control to its lending and aid as well.[19] The United States also pursued population control at home but only with certain populations. One in four Native American women was sterilized in the 1960s and 1970s.[20] Puerto Rico had a sterilization campaign, which received funding from the federal government and resulted in almost one-third of Puerto Rican women being sterilized.[21]

As bad as all that was, it could have been worse. Had the world gone all in on the original sustainability experts' favored policies, both the population and the economy would be frozen at 1970 levels. The world's population would be half of what it is today, global GDP per capita would be 1/12 of what it is today, and humanity would exist in a rigid centrally planned economy.

In the 1990s, sustainability morphed into what it is today, an ever-changing ideology that is largely about global warming but can include other progressive causes. The original sustainability ideology's proponents had claimed that if their warnings were not heeded, there would be mass starvation and societal collapse. Those claims were proven false. The world's population has more than doubled since the 1970s, yet the world has gotten wealthier, fewer people live in poverty, and resources have become more plentiful. In the developed world, obesity, not starvation, is a growing problem. Yet the same institutions that promoted the disproven sustainability ideology are playing lead roles in defining and promoting sustainability 2.0.

The World Economic Forum and *The Limits to Growth*

Klaus Schwab and the World Economic Forum are strong promoters of the new sustainability ideology. The popularity of sustainability in corporations and business schools largely reflects the WEF's efforts. The WEF also promoted the original sustainability ideology and is beginning to do so again.

The WEF held its second annual meeting in 1973. Aurelio Peccei, cofounder of the Club of Rome and a promoter of the original sustainability ideology, was invited to give a speech.[22] He summarized a book introduced earlier in this chapter, *The Limits to Growth*, which the Club of Rome had commissioned.[23] *The Limits to Growth* describes forecasts of the global economy and population, generated by computer models that were created by a team of MIT researchers.

The book predicted that civilization would collapse within 100 years because of pressures from population growth, with steep declines in food, industrial output, and resources beginning before 2050. To prevent this outcome, the size of the world's population had to be controlled and economic growth had to end.

The Limits to Growth extends the insights of Thomas Malthus, a British cleric and economist who made similar predictions in an essay he published in 1798.[24] Malthus reasoned that the population grew exponentially, while the supply of food grew arithmetically. The population, therefore, grows much faster than the food supply, so a growing population eventually starves. The world's population was about 1 billion when Malthus wrote his famous essay.[25] It had nearly quadrupled to 3.85 billion by the time The Limits to Growth was written.[26] During that period, humanity had gotten wealthier, contradicting Malthus's reasoning. The authors of The Limits to Growth ignored these facts when they made their projections.

It has been 50 years since The Limits to Growth was published. How have its prognostications held up? Since The Limits to Growth was published in 1972, the world's population has more than doubled. Yet GDP per capita has increased 12-fold since then.[27] No country over the past 50 years has had its population increase and its GDP per capita decline. In the United States and other developed countries, obesity, not lack of food, is a major health concern. In 1970, there were 1.64 billion people living in extreme poverty, while at the end of 2022 there were 648 million, a 60 percent reduction.[28]

The Limits to Growth predicted that by now we should have run out of a number of important natural resources, including petroleum, natural gas, tin, tungsten, molybdenum, and zinc. Yet we have not run out of any of these resources. In contrast, 50 years later, these resources are now more abundant than when the book was published. The world has yet to run out of a vital natural resource.

Despite all this, the WEF still promotes *The Limits to Growth* and its ideas. On its website, the WEF describes Peccei's 1973 speech as "A prescient warning on the environment."[29] The word "prescient" is defined as "having knowledge of things or events before they exist or happen." Yet *The Limits to Growth* has been wrong on its predictions.

In June 2022, the WEF published an article titled "Degrowth: What's behind the Economic Theory and Why Does It Matter Right Now?"[30] According to the article, "degrowth" means having negative economic growth as a goal. In other words, we should strive for indefinite recessions. The article says that, because of climate change, the "degrowth debate has accelerated" and that to combat global warming, "The solution is essentially to move away from the assumption that growth is good."

Notice how the emergency has changed but the "solution" remains the same? Previously, the claim was that a population emergency was imminent and required central control over the economy and a loss of personal freedom. Now the claim is that a global warming emergency is imminent and might also require abandoning the market economy and relinquishing personal freedoms to save ourselves.

The Bet: Is Economic Growth Sustainable?

In 1977, Paul Ehrlich, a Stanford biology professor, and John Holdren, a University of California, Berkeley energy professor, published a textbook, *Ecoscience*, along with Anne Ehrlich. It argued that the planet did not have enough resources to support the population, so we should strive for zero economic growth and zero population growth.[31] In *Ecoscience* they write:

> It is by now abundantly clear that the GNP (gross national product) cannot grow forever. Why should it? Why should we not strive for zero economic growth and zero population growth?[32]

This is the same logic found in *The Limits to Growth*. *Ecoscience* held up communist China and its one-child policy as "An Apparent Success Story."[33] Its authors failed to notice that throughout their entire lives the world's population had been growing, and living standards had been improving. This trend has continued over the 46 years since *Ecoscience* was first published.

Paul Ehrlich is famous for another book, *The Population Bomb*, published in 1968.[34] It predicted that in the 1970s, hundreds of millions of people would starve to death. In later editions of the book, Ehrlich predicted that this mass starvation would happen in the 1980s. In 1970, to help celebrate Earth Day, he predicted that between 1980 and 1989, some 4 billion people, including 65 million Americans, would perish in the "Great Die-Off."[35] Ehrlich became a celebrity. He went on the *Tonight Show Starring Johnny Carson* more than 20 times.[36] Ehrlich's popularity and rhetoric dovetailed with the sterilization campaigns and population control policies described earlier in this chapter.

Julian Simon, an economist, disagreed with Ehrlich's claims. Simon thought that economic growth could go on indefinitely, because growth is driven by innovation and greater innovation is always possible. Simon believed that people are the world's most valuable resource, because people can come up with new ideas that lead to innovations. Simon wrote:

> The standard of living has risen along with the size of the world's population since the beginning of recorded time. . . . There is no convincing economic reason why these trends toward a better life should not continue indefinitely.[37]

Simon also knew that prices are forward-looking. He understood Finance 101. *Future scarcity is reflected in today's prices.* If we expect greater future scarcity of a resource, its price will reflect that expectation today. If suppliers know they can sell a resource at a high price in the future, they won't sell it at a low price today. The price of a resource today must be such that sellers are indifferent between selling the resource now and in the future. Thus, if Ehrlich, Holdren, and the other sustainability ideologues were right and the world was running out of resources, that should have been reflected in current prices, but it was not.

A high price creates positive NPV investments for projects that can make the resource more plentiful. Prices guide capital to where society needs it most. If a resource has a high price, meaning high demand relative to supply, firms are incentivized to develop new supplies of the resource, develop new methods and technologies that use the resource more efficiently, and find substitutes for the resource that are more plentiful. A skeptic might ask how well this works in practice. I would ask that skeptic to name a vital resource that we have run out of.

In that spirit, Simon challenged Ehrlich to a bet. Ehrlich and a team of environmentalists, chosen by Ehrlich, could choose any five natural resources, and Simon would bet them that the prices of the resources would not rise over the next 10 years. John Holdren joined Ehrlich's team. They made the bet in September 1980. Ehrlich lost on all five commodities, which ended up with lower prices in 10 years' time. In 1990, Ehrlich paid Simon $576.07, which reflected the fact that on average the prices had fallen by 57.6 percent.[38]

This outcome was not by chance. Resources across the board have been becoming more plentiful, rather than being depleted. The website HumanProgress.org tracks commodity prices with a "time index." Each year, the nominal price of a commodity is divided by the nominal hourly income. The idea is to measure how many hours of work are needed to acquire a unit of a commodity. Every commodity that HumanProgress.org tracks has a lower *time price* today than in 1980. On average, commodity time prices have fallen by 72.3 percent since 1980.[39]

Redefining Sustainability and the Birth of ESG

In the 1990s, the United Nations and the World Bank decided to switch gears away from sterilization and population control. They decided that economic growth could continue, but only if done "sustainably." They then sought to redefine sustainability with help from "sustainability experts."

In 1995, the United Nations and the World Bank held a conference with the goal of defining sustainability. In the published conference proceedings, "Defining and Measuring Sustainability: The Biogeophysical Foundations," the lead article was written by none other than Paul Ehrlich and John Holdren, along with Gretchen C. Daily. Their article does not answer how, in practice, sustainability should be defined and measured. It does suggest that there are too many people in the world and that the world is running out of resources. What is different in this article compared with their earlier writings is that Ehrlich and Holdren are less specific about when the events will happen. This lack of specificity makes it easier for them to move the goalposts when reality does not match their predictions.[40]

Julian Simon was not asked by the World Bank or the UN for his views on sustainable development. Yet the results from their bet showed that Simon knew far more about the topic than did Ehrlich and Holdren, who had been claiming for more than two decades that any continued development was unsustainable—and were proven wrong. Why would the UN and World Bank ask Ehrlich and Holdren for their views, but not Simon?

In Simon's worldview, there is no impending global catastrophe for the UN and World Bank to solve. Capitalism takes care of things. Yet the UN and World Bank exist because supposedly there are global problems that national governments and capitalism can't address, but the UN and World Bank can. Simon's worldview is not helpful to these institutions' importance and funding. In contrast, the doomsday predictions of Ehrlich and Holdren are helpful to both organizations, giving them purpose.

Although Ehrlich and Holdren are not good economists, they are geniuses, at least according to the MacArthur Foundation. In 1990, the year in which Ehrlich lost the bet, the foundation named him a MacArthur Fellow (known informally as a genius award), which included a $345,000 payment. Holdren had already been named a MacArthur Fellow in 1981. For Ehrlich's award, the MacArthur Foundation noted the following:

> While a leader in biological research, Ehrlich also combines scientific research on population biology with public policy research to promote greater understanding of environmental problems.[41]

Julian Simon was never named a MacArthur Fellow.

Today, both the UN and World Bank play major roles in promoting ESG and in telling the world what is sustainable and what is not. As discussed in the two previous chapters, the UN played a central role in forming the fund manager and banker consortiums that are trying to enforce the agenda of net zero CO_2 emissions by 2050.

The ESG moniker can also be traced to the UN. The idea that corporations should strive to meet the social and environmental goals that the UN favors, which is not a bad description of ESG, was introduced at the 1999 Davos World Economic Forum meeting by the then-UN General Secretary Kofi Annan.[42] This idea ultimately led to the creation of the ESG moniker. The UN has since issued its "Principles for Responsible Investment," which encourage fund managers to "incorporate ESG issues into investment analysis and decision-making processes[,] . . . seek appropriate disclosure on ESG issues by the entities in which we invest[, and] . . . promote acceptance and implementation of the Principles within the investment industry."[43]

The World Bank does its part with its Global Program on Sustainability and by providing country-level ESG data. It also encourages financial institutions to consider its ESG metrics when evaluating a nation's debt.[44] A country may find it more expensive to borrow if it is not striving to meet the environmental and social policies that the World Bank tracks. Fortunately, population control and sterilizing poor people are not among the World Bank's current metrics.

We need to ask ourselves whether it is a good idea for the World Economic Forum, United Nations, and World Bank to have so much influence over our environmental and social policies. The bureaucrats who run these institutions are not elected by anyone. You cannot vote them out of office. Klaus Schwab has been at the helm of the World Economic Forum for 52 years, longer than Fidel Castro ruled Cuba. All these institutions have histories of promoting policies that disrespect basic human rights. Does it get any worse than encouraging governments to force sterilizations and abortions on their citizens?

"Sustainable Business" Is an Oxymoron

Today, the United Nations, World Bank, and World Economic Forum are at the forefront of promoting "sustainability" in the business world. Yet sustainability is a misleading term when attached to any modern business or business process. If we believe the original sustainability ideology, then economic growth is not sustainable, and a business cannot be both growing and sustainable. If we take the position that Simon and many economists do, which is that economic growth can go on indefinitely, the word "sustainability" still has no place in business parlance. Sustainable economic growth requires having businesses and business practices that are constantly being created and destroyed; none can be sustainable over the long run.

As discussed in Chapter 6, long-run economic growth is driven by innovation—no innovation, no long-run economic growth. Innovation means new things replace old things. The economist Joseph Schumpeter explained eight decades ago that creative destruction is the essential fact—that is, the central driving force—of capitalism. New firms destroy old firms. Within firms, new processes replace old ones. An economy can only continue to grow if there is creative destruction occurring continuously within it. The label "sustainable" for a firm or business process suggests that some firms and business processes can go on indefinitely, others cannot, and the labeler can tell which is which. Yet in a growing economy, no firm or business practice goes on indefinitely. Everything eventually gets replaced by something that is better in some way—whether in quality, price, ease of distribution, or other criteria as determined by consumers making free decisions in the marketplace.

The current sustainability label is often awarded to "green energy" companies, such as those focused on wind and solar energy technologies. Yet it is not uncommon for such companies to go bankrupt. Remember Solyndra? It was the solar company that got $535 million in federal loan guarantees from the Obama administration. It was supposedly a sustainable company, yet it needed federal subsidies to survive, and then it went bankrupt. Solyndra was one of 23 "sustainable energy" companies that received subsidies from the Obama administration and subsequently went bankrupt.[45] If a business is sustainable, then why does it need subsidies, and why does it go bankrupt even after receiving subsidies?

Calling something "sustainable" does not make it so. Firms that cannot make consistent profits have short lifespans. It doesn't matter if they are making solar panels, putting up windmills, or pumping oil. The irony is that ExxonMobil, which is supposedly an unsustainable business, pays billions of dollars in taxes every year. Those tax dollars are used to subsidize wind and solar companies, which are supposedly sustainable yet need government subsidies to survive. I am not knocking solar and wind energy companies. Some of them may turn out to be great businesses, but many will not. A high chance of failure is a basic feature of any innovative business or business sector. The sustainability label is given to wind and solar companies because the labelers want the world to use wind and solar energy.

We have no idea which energies future generations will use. No one knows what innovations in energy generation will occur over the next century. Perhaps the future favors nuclear power. Or perhaps we'll find ways to use fossil fuels without the side effects. Or maybe an alternative comes along that no one has thought of yet. Do you think we have discovered all the possible ways to generate energy? That is why many economists favor a carbon tax over subsidizing individual businesses and industries.[46] A carbon tax encourages companies to lower their CO_2 emissions but doesn't dictate how to accomplish that. It encourages profit-seeking firms to search for the most efficient solution. The solution may end up being wind and solar, or it may be something else.

If we want to make statements about whether a firm is likely to survive in the near term, we can use models that estimate the probability of bankruptcy.[47] These models show that the likelihood of survival is unsurprisingly higher for firms that generate consistent profits. If we want to make statements about the long run, no business survives in a growing economy that is characterized by creative destruction.

Capitalism Is Sustainable

Let's take the original sustainability ideology seriously. We have a scarce resource with a known supply and a known usage rate. With those two variables, we can attempt to forecast when we will run out of the resource. For example, if we have five million units of the resource, and we use one million units of the resource per year, we will run out in five years.

How should society deal with this? Here are four policies that might help:

1. Use the resource only if the product creates something of greater value for society.
2. Try to find substitutes that are more plentiful.
3. Invest in the development of technologies that can enable us to use the resource more efficiently. For example, instead of using one million units per year, perhaps a new technology can enable us to use only half a million units per year.
4. Try to find and develop new supplies of the resource.

Those policies are also the ones that you end up with naturally in a market economy with profit-seeking firms. If a resource is scarce, its price will be high. How do profit-seeking firms respond to this?

1. Firms will only use the resource if they can create a product that is of greater value to society. Put differently, firms will only use the resource if it helps them make a profit.
2. Firms will seek out less expensive substitutes for the resource and increase their profits.
3. Firms will try to develop ways to use the resource more efficiently. This, too, can increase their profits.
4. Firms will try to find and develop new supplies of the resource because it can be profitable.

Notice there is no mention in this list of population control, ESG ratings, or other sustainability metrics, which contribute nothing to solving the problem of how to best use scarce resources. Capitalism already has the right incentives in place for that solution. We don't need "experts" to tell us how to use resources and prevent disasters. Prices and incentives do that for us. We know from our experiment with communist central planning that when experts decide how society should use its resources, things don't go well. As the physicist David Deutsch explains:

> So there is no resource-management strategy that can prevent disasters. . . . But there are ideas that can cause disasters, and one of them is, notoriously, the idea that the future can be scientifically planned.[48]

At the core of the sustainability ideology is skepticism about innovation. Paul Ehrlich, John Holdren, the Club of Rome, and others all have long believed that society's—that is, the human mind's—ability to innovate is more limited than it has turned out to be. The original sustainability ideology essentially assumes that people are like rabbits. If there are too many rabbits in a fixed space, they eat all the plants and starve to death. But people are not like rabbits. We have more than just stomachs that consume; we also have brains that think creatively and hands that produce.[49] Humans can live in a capitalist economy with prices that reflect scarcity and firms that seek profits. In such an economy, scarcity creates a profitable opportunity for a firm that can introduce the right innovation.

How far can innovation go? Are we nearing the end of the possibilities? I'll return to an insight by the economist Paul Romer, who points out that the upper bound on innovation is all the different ways that we can combine atoms. Everything in the universe is made of atoms. Different combinations of atoms create different things. Romer teaches us that:

> The periodic table contains about a hundred different types of atoms. If a recipe is simply an indication of whether an element is included or not, there will be 100 × 99 recipes like the one for bronze or steel that involve only two elements. For recipes that

can have four elements, there are $100 \times 99 \times 98 \times 97$ recipes, which is more than 94 million. With up to 5 elements, more than 9 billion. Mathematicians call this increase in the number of combinations "combinatorial explosion. . . . As you keep going, it becomes obvious that there have been too few people on earth and too little time since we showed up, for us to have tried more than a minuscule fraction of all the possibilities.[50]

We are not even close to the end of innovation. We are at the very beginning. We have barely scratched the surface. Profits give us the incentive to keep innovating. The threat to humanity and economic growth is not scarce resources. The threat to humanity is overconfident people with a poor understanding of economics possessing large amounts of unchecked power.

CONCLUSION

Can capitalism survive? No. I do not think it can.[1]

—*Joseph Schumpeter*

The case for shareholder capitalism is not about making shareholders rich at the expense of everyone else. It does not involve zero-sum games. It has nothing to do with Wall Street. Shareholder capitalism is about mutually beneficial trading. Mutually beneficial trading is good, and more of it is better. It leads to specialization, innovation, and economic growth.

Mutually beneficial trading happens naturally. Two parties don't agree to trade unless each side expects to benefit. People have been trading in that way since the very beginning. The oldest evidence of trade is more than 300,000 years old. Apparently, trade is important for our species' survival. How long do you think you could survive without having other people to trade with?

Trade enables specialization. Instead of making everything we need ourselves, we focus on producing one thing and trade for the rest. Specialization results in society having more goods and services of higher quality.

A business is a person or group of people who specialize in trading a particular good or service. A corporation is a modern business with certain legal protections that encourage people to invest in businesses. More businesses mean more opportunities for mutually beneficial trading, which benefits us all.

Publicly traded corporations can have millions of shareholders. In this case, the shareholders cannot collectively operate the business. They hire professional managers to do that for them. The CEO and other corporate managers are employees who work for the shareholders. The one thing all the shareholders have in common is that they prefer more wealth to less. The job of corporate managers, therefore, is to maximize shareholder value. This is shareholder capitalism in practice. It offers a clear and singular goal for the corporate manager.

Much of the criticism of shareholder capitalism stems from a misunderstanding of what it means to operate a business with the goal of maximizing shareholder value. One common criticism of shareholder capitalism is that it causes corporate managers to overlook other stakeholders, such as customers, suppliers, and employees, but that notion is false. Stakeholders don't trade with a corporation unless they benefit. In a free society, trading is optional. Two parties agree to trade only if it is mutually beneficial.

Another common criticism of shareholder capitalism is that it causes managers to have a short-term focus. People who promote this idea seem to think that creating wealth for shareholders means maximizing short-term profits. Within the first couple of weeks of Finance 101, an attentive student should be able to tell you why that is wrong. In shareholder capitalism, the manager's job is to maximize shareholder value, which is a function of all the firm's expected future profits. Today's profit typically matters little for a firm's value, whereas long-term profits play the primary role. Firms regularly make investments that lower short-term profits in exchange for greater long-term profits. Shareholder capitalism requires managers to focus on the long-run success of the business.

How does shareholder capitalism fit into the bigger picture of the economy? The central problem that every society faces is how to make the best use of scarce resources that have alternative uses. What goods and services should we make? Just as importantly, what goods and services should we not make? Profits give us the answer. A profit reflects what consumers are willing to pay for a good or service, minus the cost of creating that good or service. A profit means that the value of what a firm created is greater than the value of the resources it used. When a firm makes a profit, the economy grows and society is made better off. When firms are governed by profit seeking, society has a de facto rule that says, "Only use resources to create goods and services that are more valuable than the resources being used."

Making profits is not easy. Businesses often create losses. The shareholders own those losses, too. Shareholder capitalism is fine with this fact. It is just as important for shareholders to suffer when firms fail as it is for them to prosper when firms succeed. Shareholders should get wealthier only if their firms create goods and services that benefit society. If a firm is using valuable resources but not creating goods and services that are of a greater value, then the firm is harming society. Financial losses are an incentive to stop firms from engaging in such wasteful actions.

A firm may generate losses in the short run but still be valuable if it is expected to earn profits in the future. In the long run, however, if a company remains unprofitable, it is consuming resources that could be put to better use elsewhere in the economy. It is better for both the shareholders and society if such firms die.

Shareholder capitalism can therefore be described as *pro-business*, but it does not favor any *particular business*. Shareholder capitalism encourages firms with valuable growth opportunities to invest and grow and, by doing so, it causes other firms to die. Eventually, every firm dies. Shareholder capitalism is fine with this. In a healthy economy, firms are always being born, and firms are always dying.

The case for shareholder capitalism is not a case against any other institution. Governments, universities, churches, schools, and other types of nonprofits can all play positive roles in society. Shareholder capitalism doesn't suggest otherwise. A person can have progressive political views and still be in favor of shareholder capitalism. There is no reason why a person who favors progressive taxes, a strong safety net, and strict environmental regulations cannot be in favor of shareholder capitalism. The case for shareholder capitalism isn't a case against those things. Rather, it is the recognition that it's best for society if corporations pursue profits, while other institutions do the things that corporations are not well suited for.

Corporate Social Responsibility

Corporate social responsibility is an ideological label that a person or group of people places on a business or business practice. It is ideological labeling and nothing more. Who gets to decide what is socially responsible? Anyone can. We don't hold elections for this. All someone has to do is claim that he speaks for society and begin issuing labels and edicts. Corporate social responsibility is no more than unelected persons deciding that society needs them to label things and invent rules.

When a corporation's assets are used to promote a purpose other than creating wealth for shareholders, it's a form of expropriation. Labeling an expropriation as "socially responsible" doesn't change what it is. If a corporation were to engage in a business deal that reduced the value of the corporation but financially benefited a director, the CEO, or a large shareholder, it would be illegal in the United States and in almost every other country. Yet we turn a blind eye to expropriation that funds ideological causes. Business practices that divert resources away from creating profits not only make shareholders poorer but can also affect other stakeholders, by reducing goods, services, jobs, and tax revenues.

Corporate social responsibility edicts can harm democracy. They can place different restrictions on products, services, and business practices than regulations do. Our regulatory process is far from perfect, but at least laws and regulations stem from elected officials. When enough firms follow corporate social responsibility edicts, the edicts become de facto regulations. Society is then governed by corporate social responsibility edicts and not the laws and regulations issued by the government that people voted for.

What Happens in the End?

I have no idea how all of this will play out. Here is what I think we can learn from the past, though. We have a good thing going. For the longest time, there was no economic growth. There were not enough meaningful innovations to significantly change the standard of living. The average person in 1800 lived little better materially than the average person in 100,000 B.C.[2] The amount of consumption per person was the same over that period. There may have been some differences across societies and over time, but there was no upward trend in the standard of living. GDP per capita was, for the most part, unchanged. People living in the Stone Age had the same life expectancy as people living in 1800.

Around 1800 in England, it all began to change. Driven by innovation, economic growth began. Today, people living in some developed economies are more than 20 times richer than people living in the 1800s.[3] Why economic growth began around 1800 and why it began in England are difficult questions. Some economic historians argue that property rights and English common law are important. Others argue that innovation had been occurring for centuries on a small scale, and it just happened to reach critical mass around 1800. Others point to a confluence around this time of globalization, the industrial research laboratory, and the modern corporation.[4] These explanations are not mutually exclusive, so perhaps all of them play some role.

What we do know is that prolonged economic growth requires capitalism. There is no example to the contrary. All the places that have grown and prospered since the Industrial Revolution embraced some form of capitalism, including Western Europe, the United States, Japan and South Korea after World War II, Singapore, Hong Kong, and China after it instituted its reforms. All the places that tried to end capitalism—the Soviet Union, Mao's China, East Germany, North Korea, and others— did not enjoy nearly the level of economic growth as did the more capitalist economies. All the evidence tells us that if we want economic growth, we need capitalism.

So why did Joseph Schumpeter predict that capitalism would not survive? Capitalism creates wealth, and wealth creates a class of people, the intellectual class, to which Schumpeter belonged. It largely consists of people, including me, who work in academia, media, government, and at various nonprofits. Members of the intellectual class tend to hold progressive views and dislike capitalism. Intellectuals have been attacking capitalism since at least Jean Jacques Rousseau's *Discourse on Inequality*, which was published in 1775.

The pattern is always the same. Intellectuals claim that capitalism creates problems and that they have the solutions. The solutions always require some amount of authoritarian control. Karl Marx and his followers are an example. The communists argued that capitalism was unsustainable and would eventually cause the economy and society to collapse. Communism was the only solution. Some countries went down this road and killed millions of their own people doing so. There is no example of a successful communist country. Fortunately, the world has largely turned away from communism.

Then came the original sustainability ideology. It was promoted by scientists at Stanford, Berkeley, and MIT, and by major international organizations, including the United Nations, World Bank, and World Economic Forum. The promoters claimed that the world was overpopulated, when the population was half of what it is today, and that economic growth had to end. If we didn't heed their warnings, they claimed, there would be mass starvation and society would collapse. This fear mongering went on for decades, and led to millions of forced abortions and sterilizations. Yet it could have been worse. Had the world completely bought into this ideology, the world's population would be half what it is today, and people would be controlled by a rigid central planning regime.

The intellectual class has now moved on to manipulating corporations. Here again, the claim is that capitalism is unsustainable and creating all sorts of problems. Corporations supposedly need guidance from intellectuals, who claim to know the answers to everything, including what is an appropriately diverse workforce, a fair wage, a fair trade, what is good and bad for the planet, which fuels we should use, how much CEOs should make, how much firms should invest, and so on. Like their predecessors, today's intellectuals believe they have good ideas and want to be important. Yet the track record of rule by the intellectual class is terrible—it includes totalitarianism, mass starvation, and forced sterilizations.

No system is perfect, but democracy and free trade appear to be our best bet. We don't need to add a third mechanism that gives intellectuals, or any other group of unelected persons, an outsized role in determining how we govern ourselves. We should instead protect democracy and free trade and try to prove Schumpeter wrong for as long as we can.

ACKNOWLEDGMENTS

I was fortunate to have the Cato Institute as the book's publisher. I had never published a book or even written for the general public, and I benefited greatly from the dedicated editorial team at Cato. Ivan Osorio carefully read the manuscript multiple times, always coming back with thoughtful suggestions that improved the book on multiple fronts. Aaron Steelman and Jeff Miron provided valuable comments. Aaron also solicited helpful feedback from several reviewers. I thank Marcy Gessel, Karen Ingebretsen, and Kay McCarthy of Publications Professionals LLC for attentive copy editing. I am grateful to Eleanor O'Connor for shepherding the book through the editorial process and on to publication.

I was lucky to have Alex Edmans review an early draft of the book. Alex is a successful book author who has written extensively on many of the topics this book covers. What better person to get feedback from? He generously gave encouraging and thoughtful comments that led to significant improvements.

S. P. Kothari also saw an early draft of the book and provided insightful comments. In particular, S. P.'s feedback improved the exposition in several chapters, which made the final product much better.

I am grateful to my colleagues at Georgetown University and other finance academics for discussions that deepened my understanding of the book's subject matter. Conversations about the publication process with Jeffrey Pontiff and Sean Flynn were extremely helpful. I could not have completed this book without the support of my employer, the McDonough School of Business at Georgetown, which gave me the necessary time and freedom.

Finally, I can't recall how many times I asked Mengxin Zhao, my wife, for her opinion on some aspect of the book. One of the benefits of having a wife with a PhD in finance who does research on corporate governance is that you can lean on her when writing a book about shareholder capitalism. I must also thank Mengxin and our children, Ethan and Evelyn, for putting up with my obsession with this book over the past year.

NOTES

Introduction

[1] Adam Smith, *An Inquiry into the Nature and Causes of the Wealth of Nations*, bk. 1, chap. 2 (London: printed for PW. Strahan and T. Cadell, 1776; Carmel, Indiana: Liberty Fund, Inc., 1981), p. 26.

[2] The findings are documented in three related studies: Alan Deino et al., "Chronology of the Acheulean to Middle Stone Age Transition in Eastern Africa," *Science* 360, no. 6384 (March 2018): 95–98; Richard Potts et al., "Environmental Dynamics during the Onset of the Middle Stone Age in Eastern Africa," *Science* 360, no. 6384 (March 2018): 86–90; and Richard Potts et al., "Environmental Dynamics during the Onset of the Middle Stone Age in Eastern Africa," *Science Advances* 6, no. 43 (October 2020). The following articles summarize the three studies: Lauren Boissoneault, "Colored Pigments and Complex Tools Suggest Humans Were Trading 100,000 Years Earlier Than Previously Believed," *Smithsonian Magazine*, March 15, 2018; and Alina Polianskaya, "Humans May Have Been Trading with Each Other as Far Back as 300,000 Years," *inews*, March 15, 2018.

[3] Nick Blegen, "The Earliest Long-Distance Obsidian Transport: Evidence from the ~200 ka Middle Stone Age Sibilo School Road Site, Baringo, Kenya," *Journal of Human Evolution* 103 (February 2017): 1–19.

[4] Archaeological evidence is consistent with both within-group and across-group trading among humans but not Neanderthals, who lived in small groups that did not interact. Richard D. Horan, Erwin Bulte, and Jason Shogren, "How Trade Saved Humanity from Biological Exclusion:

An Economic Theory of Neanderthal Extinction," *Journal of Economic Behavior & Organization* 58, no. 1 (2005): 1–29.

[5] Joshua J. Mark, "Uruk," in *World History Encyclopedia*, last modified April 28, 2011, https://www.worldhistory.org/uruk/.

[6] "Where Was the First City in the World?" *New Scientist*.

[7] Denise Schmandt-Besserat, "The Evolution of Writing," *International Encyclopedia of Social and Behavioral Sciences* (2014): 1–15; The Editors, "The World's Oldest Writing," *Archaeology*, May/June 2016; and Alex Bridget, "What the Earliest Texts Say about the Invention of Writing," *Discover Magazine*, January 2, 2019.

[8] Smith, *An Inquiry into the Nature and Causes of the Wealth of Nations*. The Adam Smith Institute provides a helpful condensed version of *Wealth of Nations*. Eamonn Butler is the author of *The Condensed Wealth of Nations and the Incredibly Condensed Theory of Moral Sentiments,* published in 2011.

[9] Milton Friedman, "The Social Responsibility of Business Is to Increase Its Profits," *New York Times Magazine*, September 13, 1970.

[10] For a discussion of recent academic research on this topic see Hao Liang and Phong Nguyen, "Social Responsibility in Business and Finance," in *Handbook of Financial Decision Making*, edited by Gilles Hilary and R. David McLean (Cheltenham, UK: Edward Elgar Publishing, 2023).

[11] The principle of shareholder value maximization is also defended in Richard M. Frankel, S.P. Kothari, and Lou Zuo, *The Economics of Accounting* (Oxford, UK: Oxford University Press, forthcoming), and Diane Denis, "Corporate Governance and the Goal of the Firm: In Defense of Shareholder Wealth Maximization," *Financial Review* 51, no. 4 (2016): 467-480. The book *Grow the Pie* also studies shareholder capitalism and some of the controversies that surround it. Alex Edmans, *Grow the Pie* (Cambridge, UK: Cambridge University Press, 2022).

[12] The concept of corporate social responsibility can be traced to E. Merrick Dodd Jr., "For Whom Are Corporate Managers Trustees?," *Harvard Law Review* 45, no. 7 (1932): 1145–63; and Howard R. Bowen, *Social Responsibilities of the Businessman* (Iowa City: University of Iowa Press, 1953). For a discussion on this topic, see Archie B. Carroll, "A History of Corporate Social Responsibility: Concepts and Practices," in *The Oxford Handbook of Corporate Social Responsibility*, ed. Andrew Crane et al. (Oxford, UK: Oxford University Press, 2008).

[13] This statistic is from QuantGov, Mercatus Center at George Mason University, Arlington, VA: https://www.quantgov.org/federal-us-tracker.

[14] John W. Dawson and John J. Seater, "Federal Regulation and Aggregate Economic Growth," *Journal of Economic Growth* 18 (2013): 137-177; and Joseph Kalmenovitz, "Regulatory Intensity and Firm-Specific Exposure," *Review of Financial Studies* 36, no. 8 (August 2023):3311-3347.

[15] In theory, if people agree on what the costs and benefits are, then they can agree on the optimal policy. In practice, people often disagree over the costs and benefits of various policies. For example, I might care more about the environment and you might care more about economic growth. Each of us would each prefer different environmental regulations, because stricter environmental regulations can limit growth.

[16] Jean-Jacques Rousseau, *A Discourse on Inequality*, trans. Maurice Cranston (London: Penguin Books, 1985).

Chapter 1

[1] Thomas Sowell, *Basic Economics: A Citizens Guide to the Economy* (New York: Basic Books, 2000).

[2] This statistic is from the Bureau of Labor Statistics: https://www.bls.gov/bdm/us_age_naics_00_table7.txt.

[3] This statistic is from QuantGov, Mercatus Center at George Mason University, Arlington, VA: https://www.quantgov.org/federal-us-tracker.

[4] Steven Eder, "When Picking Apples on a Farm with 5,000 Rules, Watch Out for the Ladder," *New York Times*, December 27, 2017.

[5] These statistics are from the Bureau of Labor Statistics: https://www.bls.gov/bdm/us_age_naics_00_table7.txt.

Chapter 2

[1] Alex Edmans, "Why Shareholder Capitalism Benefits Wider Society," VoxEU column, May 26, 2021.

[2] If you invest $1 for one year and expect a return of 7 percent, then the *future value* is $1 × 1.07 = $1.07. If the expected rate of return is 7 percent, then 7 percent is the discount rate, and 1.07 is the discount factor that we can use to find *present value*. The present value of $1.07 using a

7 percent expected return = $1.07/1.07 = $1. The present value of $10 using a 7 percent expected return = $10/1.07 = $9.35. If you invest $9.35 for one year and earn 7 percent, you end up with $10: $9.35 × 1.07 = $10. We can do this for multiple years, too. The future value of $1 invested at 7 percent for two years = $1 × 1.07 × 1.07 = $1 × $1.07^2 = $1.145. The discount factor for this horizon is then 1.07^2. The present value of $1.145 received in two years is $1.145/1.07^2 = $1.

[3] In practice, the Capital Asset Pricing Model, or CAPM, is often used to estimate the firm's riskiness and discount rate.

[4] Mary Jo White, chair of the U.S. Securities and Exchange Commission, "The Path Forward on Disclosure" (speech to National Association of Corporate Directors, October 15, 2013).

Chapter 3

[1] Adam Smith, *An Inquiry into the Nature and Causes of the Wealth of Nations*, bk 4, chap. 2 (London: printed for W. Strahan and T. Cadell, 1776; Carmel, Indiana: Liberty Fund, Inc., 1981), p. 421.

Chapter 4

[1] Paul M. Romer, "Economic Growth," Econlib, Library of Economics and Liberty website.

[2] Paul Romer, "The Deep Structure of Economic Growth," PaulRomer.net, February 5, 2019.

[3] Robert M. Solow, "Technical Change and the Aggregate Production Function," *Review of Economics and Statistics* (1957): 312–20.

[4] Judith Z. Kalbacher and D. DeAre, "Farm Population of the United States, 1985," *Current Population Reports, Series P-20, Population Characteristics* 59 (1986): i–20.

[5] Economic Research Service, U.S. Department of Agriculture, "Ag and Food Sectors and the Economy," USDA website.

[6] Paul Romer, "The Deep Structure of Economic Growth."

[7] Paul M. Romer, "Endogenous Technological Change," *Journal of Political Economy* 98, no. 5 (1990): S71–102.

[8] Zain Rizvi, "The NIH Vaccine," Public Citizen, June 25, 2020.

[9] For an example, see John Abramson, *Sickening: How Big Pharma Broke American Health Care and How We Can Replace It* (New York: Mariner Books, 2023).

[10] William D. Nordhaus, "Schumpeterian Profits in the American Economy: Theory and Measurement," National Bureau of Economic Research Working Paper no. 10433, April 2004.

[11] Nordhaus, "Schumpeterian Profits in the American Economy," p. 4.

Chapter 5

[1] James R. Brown, Gustav Martinsson, and Bruce C. Petersen, "Law, Stock Markets, and Innovation," *Journal of Finance* 68, no. 4 (2013): 1517–49.

[2] A good deal of research shows that stock markets are more important for funding innovation than credit markets. For an example, see Brown, Martinsson, and Petersen, "Law, Stock Markets, and Innovation."

[3] Anthony Di Pizio, "If You Had Invested $10,000 in Tesla Stock at Its IPO, Here Is How Much You'd Have Today," The Motley Fool, December 21, 2022.

[4] If you played the game 100 times it would cost you $100 × 100 = $10,000. The 10 wins would yield you $1,100 × 10 = $11,000. Your profit from the 100 games = $11,000 − $10,000 = $1,000. Your rate of return = $1,000/$10,000 = 10 percent.

[5] Typically, firms in the same industry will have returns that are correlated as they face similar risks. What is different here is that we are assuming that these innovative firms are betting on different technologies and thus face different and uncorrelated risks.

[6] The variance for investing in one firm = $0.1 × (10 − 0.1)^2 + 0.9 × (−1 − 0.1)^2 = 1,089$ percent. If there is no correlation among the assets, then the variance of a portfolio can be written as $\sigma^2 = \sum_{i=1}^{N} w_i^2 \sigma_i^2$, where σ^2 is variance and w_i denotes the weight of asset i. There are N assets in the portfolio. The portfolio's standard deviation is the square root of its variance. For the 10-asset portfolio, the variance = $10 × 0.10^2 × 1,089$ percent = 109 percent. The standard deviation is 104 percent.

[7] The expected return of the combined portfolio = 0.80 × 9.20 percent + 0.20 × 10 percent = 9.29 percent. The correlation and covariance between the S&P 500 and the innovation portfolio are both zero. The variance of the combined portfolio therefore = $0.80^2 × 2.07$ percent + $0.20^2 × 11$ percent = 1.76 percent. The combined portfolio's standard deviation is the square root of its variance = 13.28 percent.

[8] Even if there is only a small number of highly innovative firms, investors can still invest with the benefits of diversification by investing a

small amount into each firm. For example, if there is only one innovative firm, an investor could just give it a portfolio weight of 0.20 percent, as was done in Table 5.3, and the firm will not increase the portfolio's standard deviation.

Chapter 6

[1] Joseph A. Schumpeter, *Capitalism, Socialism and Democracy* (New York: Harper & Brothers, 1942).

[2] Mark J. Perry, "Only 52 U.S. Companies Have Been on the Fortune 500 since 1955, Thanks to Creative Destruction That Fuels Prosperity," *Carpe Diem* (blog), American Enterprise Institute, June 3, 2021.

[3] Kathy Fogel, Randall Morck, and Bernard Yeung, "Big Business Stability and Economic Growth: Is What's Good for General Motors Good for America?," *Journal of Financial Economics* 89, no. 1 (2008): 83–108.

[4] Richard Alm and W. Michael Cox, "Creative Destruction," Econlib, Library of Economics and Liberty website.

[5] Alm and Cox, "Creative Destruction."

[6] Steven J. Davis, John C. Haltiwanger, and Scott Schuh, *Job Creation and Destruction* (Cambridge, MA: MIT Press, 1996).

[7] These statistics are from the World Bank, https://data.worldbank.org/indicator/NY.GDP.PCAP.CD.

[8] South Dakota State Agriculture Heritage Museum, "Blacksmithing & Wagon Works," *Throwback Thursday* (blog), July 7, 2022.

Chapter 7

[1] Nikolai Shmelev and Vladimir Popov, *The Turning Point: Revitalizing the Soviet Economy*, trans. Michele A. Berdy (New York: Doubleday, 1989).

[2] Shmelev and Popov, *The Turning Point,* p. 141.

[3] Shmelev and Popov, *The Turning Point*, p. 118.

[4] John F. Burns, "Soviet Food Shortages: Grumbling and Excuses," *New York Times,* January 15, 1982.

[5] Adam Smith, *An Inquiry into the Nature and Causes of the Wealth of Nations*, bk 1, chap. 2 (London: printed for W. Strahan and T. Cadell, 1776; Carmel, Indiana: Liberty Fund, Inc., 1981), pgs. 26–27.

[6] Frank Dikötter, *Mao's Great Famine: The History of China's Most Devastating Catastrophe* (London: Bloomsbury; New York: Walker Books, 2010), p. 448.

[7] Daniel Kelliher, *Peasant Power in China: The Era of Rural Reform, 1979–1989* (New Haven, CT: Yale University Press, 1992), p. 202.

[8] Clyde D. Stoltenberg, "China's Special Economic Zones: Their Development and Prospects," *Asian Survey* 24, no. 6 (1984): 637–54, https://doi.org/10.2307/2644396.

[9] "Special Economic Zone," *Encyclopedia Britannica*, March 20, 2023.

[10] Paul Romer, "The Deep Structure of Economic Growth," PaulRomer.net, February 5, 2019.

[11] World Bank and Development Research Center of the State Council, the People's Republic of China, *Four Decades of Poverty Reduction in China: Drivers, Insights for the World, and the Road Ahead* (Washington: World Bank, 2022).

[12] Sascha O. Becker, Lukas Mergele, and Ludger Woessmann, "The Separation and Reunification of Germany: Rethinking a Natural Experiment Interpretation of the Enduring Effects of Communism," *Journal of Economic Perspectives* 34, no. 2 (2020): 143–71.

[13] Aaron O'Neill, "Population in the Former Territories of the Federal Republic of Germany and the German Democratic Republic from 1950 to 2016," Statista, June 21, 2022.

[14] O'Neill, "Population in the Former Territories."

[15] Stephen Beard, "Itemizing Germany's $2 Trillion Bill for Reunification," *Marketplace*, American Public Radio, November 5, 2019.

[16] Helena J. Merriman, "The Tunnel of Love," *Mail on Sunday*, August 1, 2021.

[17] John Hooper, "East Germany Jailed 75,000 Escapers," *The Guardian*, August 6, 2001.

[18] Hooper, "East Germany Jailed 75,000 Escapers."

[19] Ferdinand Protzman, "East Germany's Economy Far Sicker Than Expected," *New York Times*, September 20, 1990.

[20] Protzman, "East Germany's Economy."

[21] Protzman, "East Germany's Economy."

[22] Protzman, "East Germany's Economy."

[23] Protzman, "East Germany's Economy."

[24] Girard Steichen, "East Germany's Economy Totters," *Christian Science Monitor*, August 16, 1990.

[25] Stephane Courtois et al., *The Black Book of Communism: Crimes, Terror, Repression* (Cambridge, MA: Harvard University Press, 1999).

[26] Rudolph J. Rummel, *Death by Government* (Piscataway, NJ: Transaction Publishers, 1997).

Chapter 8

[1] Milton Friedman and Rose Friedman, *Free to Choose* (New York: Harcourt, Inc., 1990).

[2] Natalie Winters, "Revealed: The 'Public Figures' Attending the 2022 World Economic Forum in Davos," National Pulse, May 20, 2022.

[3] Business Standard Web Team, "WEF 2022: Over 50 Govt Heads, 1250 Leaders from Pvt Sector to Meet in Davos," *Business Standard*, May 19, 2022.

[4] Business Standard Web Team, "WEF 2022."

[5] World Economic Forum, *Annual Report 2021–2022* (Geneva, Switzerland: World Economic Forum, 2022).

[6] The WEF's partners are listed here: https://www.weforum.org/partners/#search.

[7] World Economic Forum, "A Partnership in Shaping History: 1971–2020." The WEF mentions its engagement with academia throughout this booklet that describes its history.

[8] WEF, "A Partnership in Shaping History," p. 15.

[9] WEF, "A Partnership in Shaping History," p. 254.

[10] World Economic Forum, "A Platform for Impact" (institutional brochure, WEF, Geneva, Switzerland, 2019), p. 9.

[11] Klaus Schwab, "Davos Manifesto 2020: The Universal Purpose of a Company in the Fourth Industrial Revolution," World Economic Forum, December 2, 2019.

[12] Business Roundtable, "For Long-Term Success Companies Must Deliver for All Stakeholders," press release, August 19, 2022.

[13] Business Roundtable, "Business Roundtable Redefines the Purpose of a Corporation to Promote 'An Economy That Serves All Americans,'" press release, August 19, 2019.

[14] Business Roundtable, "Our Commitment," preamble to the Statement on the Purpose of a Corporation," 2019. The person in charge of

the language of the updated statement was Johnson & Johnson CEO Alex Gorsky, who heads the Roundtable's governance committee. In an interview about the creation of the updated statement, Gorsky said, "There were times when I felt like Thomas Jefferson." David Gelles and Favid Yaffe-Bellany, "Shareholder Value Is No Longer Everything, Top CEOs Say," *New York Times,* August 19, 2019.

[15] BlackRock, "BlackRock Reports First Quarter 2023 Diluted EPS of $7.64, or $7.93 as Adjusted," press release, April 14, 2023.

[16] Larry Fink, "The Power of Capitalism," 2022 Letter to CEOs, 2022.

[17] Elizabeth Warren, "Companies Shouldn't Be Accountable Only to Shareholders," *Wall Street Journal*, August 14, 2018.

[18] These statistics are from the Bureau of Labor Statistics: https://www.bls.gov/bdm/us_age_naics_00_table7.txt.

[19] The extent of limited liability that a government should grant is a debatable issue that goes beyond the scope of this book.

[20] Elizabeth Warren, Accountable Capitalism Act one-pager. This document outlines some provisions of the Accountable Capitalism Act.

[21] Adi Ignatius, "Profits and Purpose," *Harvard Business Review*, March–April 2019, p. 10.

Chapter 9

[1] Glenn Hubbard, "Was Milton Friedman Right about Shareholder Capitalism?" (Harvard Law School Forum on Corporate Governance, Michael Strain, moderator, April 21, 2021).

[2] Peter Drucker, *The Practice of Management* (New York: Harper Business, 1993), p. 37.

[3] An example of this type of thinking was evident in the debate that surrounded the Trump administration's corporate tax cuts, with some insisting that the resulting higher profits be used to increase worker pay. See Jim Tankersley, "Will a Corporate Tax Cut Lift Worker Pay? A Union Wants It in Writing," *New York Times*, November 23, 2017.

[4] Klaus Schwab and Peter Vanham, "What Is Stakeholder Capitalism?," The Davos Agenda 2021, World Economic Forum, January 22, 2021.

[5] "Recalling Apple's VC-Funded Past," PitchBook, News and Analysis entry, September 14, 2012.

Chapter 10

[1] Richard Brealey et al., *Principles of Corporate Finance*, 14th ed. (New York: McGraw Hill, 2023), p. 119.

[2] Klaus Schwab, "A Better Economy Is Possible. But We Don't Need to Reimagine Capitalism to Do It," *Time*, October 21, 2020.

[3] Peter Vanham, "Klaus Schwab Releases 'Stakeholder Capitalism'; Making the Case for a Global Economy That Works for Progress, People and Planet," World Economic Forum press release, January 29, 2021.

[4] Vanham, "Klaus Schwab Releases 'Stakeholder Capitalism.'"

[5] Klaus Schwab and Peter Vanham, "What Is Stakeholder Capitalism?," The Davos Agenda 2021, World Economic Forum, January 22, 2021.

[6] European Commission, "Study on Directors' Duties and Sustainable Corporate Governance," prepared by EY (Luxembourg: European Union Publications Office, July 2020), Abstract.

[7] European Commission, "Study on Directors' Duties," listed as "Driver 1."

[8] European Commission, "Study on Directors' Duties," listed as "Driver 2."

[9] Alex Edmans et al., "Call for Reflection on Sustainable Corporate Governance," European Corporate Governance Institute, April 7, 2021.

[10] Alex Edmans, "Why Shareholder Capitalism Benefits Wider Society," VoxEU column, May 26, 2021.

[11] Klaus Schwab, "Davos Manifesto 2020: The Universal Purpose of a Company in the Fourth Industrial Revolution," World Economic Forum, December 2, 2019.

[12] Martin Lipton, "Was Milton Friedman Right about Shareholder Capitalism?" (Harvard Law School Forum on Corporate Governance, April 21, 2021).

[13] Lipton, "Was Milton Friedman Right?"

[14] Milton Friedman, "The Social Responsibility of Business Is to Increase Its Profits," *New York Times Magazine*, September 13, 1970.

[15] See the following studies as examples: Sheridan Titman, K. C. John Wei, and Feixue Xie, "Capital Investments and Stock Returns," *Journal of Financial and Quantitative Analysis* 39, no. 4 (2004): 677–700; Michael J. Cooper, Huseyin Gulen, and Michael J. Schill, "Asset Growth and the Cross-Section of Stock Returns," *Journal of Finance* 63, no. 4

(2008): 1609–51; Robert Novy-Marx, "The Other Side of Value: The Gross Profitability Premium," *Journal of Financial Economics* 108, no. 1 (2013): 1–28; and Ray Ball et al., "Accruals, Cash Flows, and Operating Profitability in the Cross Section of Stock Returns," *Journal of Financial Economics* 121, no. 1 (2016): 28–45.

Chapter 11

[1] Steven N. Kaplan, "Are US Companies Too Short-Term Oriented? Some Thoughts," *Journal of Applied Corporate Finance* 30, no. 4 (2018): 8–18.

[2] Professor Mark Roe has written several articles and a book that pushes back against the idea that short-termism is harming firms and the economy. Mark Roe, *Missing the Target*, (Oxford, UK: Oxford University Press, 2022).

[3] Marcia Wendorf, "Institutional Investors Explained," Seeking Alpha, May 2022.

[4] The R&D spending numbers are taken from the firms' annual reports.

[5] Richard Mille, "Forbes World's Billionaires List: The Richest in 2022," *Forbes*, 2022.

[6] Michael Sheetz, "Elon Musk's SpaceX Raised $850 Million, Jumping Valuation to about $74 Billion," CNBC, February 27, 2021.

[7] Jay Ritter, "The Long-Run Performance of Initial Public Offerings," *Journal of Finance* 46, no. 1 (1991): 3–27.

[8] These studies are numerous and have been replicated many times. The website openassetpricing.com provides computer codes and replication results from all the major studies. See the following studies as examples: Robert Novy-Marx, "The Other Side of Value: The Gross Profitability Premium," *Journal of Financial Economics* 108, no. 1 (2013): 1–28; and Ray Ball et al., "Accruals, Cash Flows, and Operating Profitability in the Cross Section of Stock Returns," *Journal of Financial Economics* 121, no. 1 (2016): 28–45.

[9] See the following studies as examples: Sheridan Titman, K. C. John Wei, and Feixue Xie, "Capital Investments and Stock Returns," *Journal of Financial and Quantitative Analysis* 39, no. 4 (2004): 677–700; and Michael J. Cooper, Huseyin Gulen, and Michael J. Schill, "Asset Growth and the Cross-Section of Stock Returns," *Journal of Finance* 63, no. 4 (2008): 1609–51.

[10] See the following studies as examples: Rafael La Porta et al., "Good News for Value Stocks: Further Evidence on Market Efficiency," *Journal of Finance* 52, no. 2 (1997): 859–74; Titman, Wei, and Xie, "Capital Investments"; Cooper, Gulen, and Schill, "Asset Growth"; and Jeffrey Pontiff and Artemiza Woodgate, "Share Issuance and Cross-Sectional Returns," *Journal of Finance* 63, no. 2 (2008): 921–45.

[11] The same studies that document overvaluation also document undervaluation. As an example, firms with high investment have relatively low stock returns, whereas firms with low investment have relatively high stock returns. See La Porta et al., "Good News"; Titman, Wei, and Xie, "Capital Investments"; Cooper, Gulen, and Schill, "Asset Growth"; and Pontiff and Woodgate, "Share Issuance."

[12] See the following studies as examples: Rafael La Porta et al., "Good News for Value Stocks: Further Evidence on Market Efficiency," *Journal of Finance* 52, no. 2 (1997): 859–74; Sheridan Titman, K. C. John Wei, and Feixue Xie, "Capital Investments and Stock Returns," *Journal of Financial and Quantitative Analysis* 39, no. 4 (2004): 677–700; Michael J. Cooper, Huseyin Gulen, and Michael J. Schill, "Asset Growth and the Cross-Section of Stock Returns," *Journal of Finance* 63, no. 4 (2008): 1609–51; and Jeffrey Pontiff and Artemiza Woodgate, "Share Issuance and Cross-Sectional Returns," *Journal of Finance* 63, no. 2 (2008): 921–45.

Chapter 12

[1] M. F. Bastiat, *What Is Seen and What Is Not Seen, or Political Economy in One Lesson* (Paris: Guillaumin, July 1850); republished on Online Library of Liberty, November 17, 2015.

[2] European Commission, "Study on Directors' Duties and Sustainable Corporate Governance," prepared by EY (Luxembourg: European Union Publications Office, July 2020), p. 9.

[3] Richard Brealey et al., *Principles of Corporate Finance*, 14th ed. (New York: McGraw Hill, 2023), p. 10.

[4] M. F. Bastiat, *What Is Seen and What Is Not Seen.*

[5] Brian Faler, "Democrats Go with 'the Least Bad' Tax, " *Politico*, August 5, 2022.

[6] "Measuring Stakeholder Capitalism: Towards Common Metrics and Consistent Reporting of Sustainable Value Creation" (White Paper, World Economic Forum, September 2020).

[7] Eugene F. Fama and Kenneth R. French, "Financing Decisions: Who Issues Stock?," *Journal of Financial Economics* 76, no. 3 (2005): 549–82; and Pontiff and Woodgate, "Share Issuance."

[8] Fama and French, "Financing Decisions"; and Pontiff and Woodgate, "Share Issuance."

[9] The paper "Short-Termism and Capital Flows" provides a nice discussion of how repurchases are not as large as some claim once share issues and other factors are accounted for. Jesse M. Fried and Charles C. Y. Wang, "Short-Termism and Capital Flows," *Review of Corporate Finance Studies* 8, no. 1 (2019): 207–233.

[10] Fama and French, "Financing Decisions"; and Pontiff and Woodgate, "Share Issuance."

[11] R. David McLean, Jeffrey Pontiff, and Akiko Watanabe, "Share Issuance and Cross-Sectional Returns: International Evidence," *Journal of Financial Economics* 94, no. 1 (2009): 1–17.

[12] Roni Michaely and Amani Moin, "Disappearing and Reappearing Dividends," *Journal of Financial Economics* 143, no. 1 (January 2022): 207–26, https://doi.org/10.1016/j.jfineco.2021.06.029.

[13] See Fama and French, "Financing Decisions"; and Michaely and Moin, "Disappearing and Reappearing Dividends;" and Amy Dittmar, "Why Do Firms Repurchase Stock?," *Journal of Business* 73, no. 3 (July 2000): 331–355; and Alex Edmans, "The Case for Stock Buybacks," *Harvard Business Review*, September 15, 2017.

[14] Alon Brav et al., "Payout Policy in the 21st Century," *Journal of Financial Economics* 77, no. 3 (2005): 483–527.

[15] Craig M. Lewis and Joshua T. White, "Corporate Liquidity Provision and Share Repurchase Programs," U.S. Chamber of Commerce Center for Capital Markets Competitiveness, Fall 2021 Report, September 24, 2021.

[16] Fama and French, "Financing Decisions."

[17] *American Lawyer* staff, "The 2021 Am Law 100: Ranked by Profits per Equity Partner," *American Lawyer*, April 20, 2021.

[18] *American Lawyer* staff, "The 2021 Am Law 100."

[19] Greg Roumeliotis, "Small Is Lucrative for Wachtell, Corporate America's Legal Defense Force," Reuters, June 8, 2017.

Chapter 13

[1] Warren Buffett letter to shareholders, February 25, 2023, Berkshire Hathaway Inc.

[2] Thomas Franck, "Elizabeth Warren Rips Stock Buybacks as Nothing but Paper Manipulation," CNBC, March 2, 2021.

[3] Charles Schumer and Bernie Sanders, "Schumer and Sanders: Limit Corporate Stock Buybacks," op-ed, *New York Times*, February 3, 2019.

[4] Robert Reich, "The Buyback Boondoggle Is Beggaring America," robertreich.org, March 19, 2018.

[5] David Ikenberry, Josef Lakonishok, and Theo Vermaelen, "Market Underreaction to Open Market Share Repurchases," *Journal of Financial Economics* 39, no. 2–3 (1995): 181–208; R. David McLean, Jeffrey Pontiff, and Akiko Watanabe, "Share Issuance and Cross-Sectional Returns: International Evidence," *Journal of Financial Economics* 94, no. 1 (2009): 1–17.

[6] Ikenberry, Lakonishok, and Vermaelen, "Market Underreaction."

[7] See the following studies as examples: Rafael La Porta et al., "Good News for Value Stocks: Further Evidence on Market Efficiency," *Journal of Finance* 52, no. 2 (1997): 859–74; Sheridan Titman, K. C. John Wei, and Feixue Xie, "Capital Investments and Stock Returns," *Journal of Financial and Quantitative Analysis* 39, no. 4 (2004): 677–700; Michael J. Cooper, Huseyin Gulen, and Michael J. Schill, "Asset Growth and the Cross-Section of Stock Returns," *Journal of Finance* 63, no. 4 (2008): 1609–51; and Jeffrey Pontiff and Artemiza Woodgate, "Share Issuance and Cross-Sectional Returns," *Journal of Finance* 63, no. 2 (2008): 921–45.

[8] Alex Edmans, Vivian W. Fang, and Allen H. Huang, "The Long-Term Consequences of Short-Term Incentives," *Journal of Accounting Research* 60, no. 3 (2022): 1007–46.

[9] Alex Edmans, "The Case for Stock Buybacks," *Harvard Business Review*, September 15, 2017; and Alex Edmans, *Grow the Pie: How Great Companies Deliver Both Purpose and Profit* (Cambridge: Cambridge University Press, 2020).

[10] See Eugene F. Fama and Kenneth R. French, "Financing Decisions: Who Issues Stock?," *Journal of Financial Economics* 76, no. 3 (2005): 549–82.

[11] Ikenberry, Lakonishok, and Vermaelen, "Market Underreaction."

Chapter 14

[1] This is somewhat of a simplification, as Musk actually owns about 85 percent of the shares and he is not the only person on the management team. Aimee Picchi, "Biden Says Elon Musk's Foreign Investors in Twitter Are 'Worth Being Looked At,'" CBS News, November 9, 2022.

[2] Megan McArdle, "Opinion: How Elon Musk Fired Twitter Staff and Broke Nothing," *Washington Post*, February 19, 2023.

[3] Martin Lipton, "Wachtell Lipton Discusses Purpose, Stakeholders, ESG, and Sustainable Long-Term Investment," *CLS Blue Sky* (blog), December 24, 2019.

[4] Corporations are recognized legally as independent entities separate from the business owners. This has been the case since at least Chief Justice John Marshall's 1819 remark that "a corporation is an artificial being, invisible, intangible, and existing only in contemplation of law." See Robert Hesson, "Corporations," Econlib. Yet, shares give the business owners control over the corporation. If a corporation is formed, the business owners can continue to operate their business as they see fit (or to sell it, or liquidate its assts) with the added benefit of limited liability.

[5] The separation of ownership and control in corporations has been studied by generations of economists, beginning with A. A. Berle Jr. and G. C. Means, *The Modern Corporation and Private Property* (New York: Macmillan, 1932). Important studies include Eugene F. Fama and Michael C. Jensen, "Separation of Ownership and Control," *Journal of Law and Economics* 26, no. 2 (1983): 301–25; and Michael C. Jensen and William H. Meckling, "Theory of the Firm: Managerial Behavior, Agency Costs and Ownership Structure," *Journal of Financial Economics* 3, no. 4 (1976): 305–60.

[6] The idea that a corporation can be compared to a republic is developed in Paul Gompers, Joy Ishii, and Andrew Metrick, "Corporate Governance and Equity Prices," *Quarterly Journal of Economics* 118, no. 1 (2003): 107–56.

[7] Simeon Djankov et al., "The Law and Economics of Self-Dealing," *Journal of Financial Economics* 88, no. 3 (2008): 430–65.

[8] As examples: Rafael La Porta et al., "Law and Finance," *Journal of Political Economy* 106, no. 6 (1998): 1113–55; Rafael La Porta et al., "Legal Determinants of External Finance," *Journal of Finance* 52, no. 3 (1997): 1131–50; Rafael La Porta et al., "Investor Protection and

Corporate Valuation," *Journal of Finance* 57, no. 3 (2002): 1147–70; R. David McLean, Tianyu Zhang, and Mengxin Zhao, "Why Does the Law Matter? Investor Protection and Its Effects on Investment, Finance, and Growth," *Journal of Finance* 67, no. 1 (2012): 313–50; and Djankov et al., "The Law and Economics of Self-Dealing."

[9] Lucian A. Bebchuk, Alma Cohen, and Scott Hirst, "The Agency Problems of Institutional Investors," *Journal of Economic Perspectives* 31, no. 3 (2017): 89–112; and Scott Hirst and Lucian Bebchuk, "The Specter of the Giant Three," *Boston University Law Review* 99, no. 3 (2019): 721.

[10] Some of the agency problems of institutional investors are discussed in Bebchuk, Cohen, and Hirst, "The Agency Problems of Institutional Investors."

Chapter 15

[1] Alon Brav, Wei Jiang, and Hyunseob Kim, "The Real Effects of Hedge Fund Activism: Productivity, Asset Allocation, and Labor Outcomes," *Review of Financial Studies* 28, no. 10 (2015): 2723–69.

[2] Vivek Ramaswamy, "Shareholders Stand Up for Profit and against ESG at Chevron," *Wall Street Journal,* September 7, 2022.

[3] Ramaswamy, "Shareholders Stand Up."

[4] Vanguard, "An Update on Vanguard's Engagement with the Net Zero Asset Managers Initiative (NAZM)," corporate statement, December 7, 2022.

[5] Regulation statistics can be found at QuantGov, Mercatus Center at George Mason University, Arlington, VA: https://www.quantgov.org/visuals.

[6] BlackRock, "iShares ESG Aware MSCI USA ETF."

[7] Cliff Asness, "Virtue Is Its Own Reward or One Man's Floor Is Another Man's Ceiling," AQR Education, May 18, 2017.

[8] Florian Berg, Julian F. Koelbel, and Roberto Rigobon, "Aggregate Confusion: The Divergence of ESG Ratings," *Review of Finance* 26, no. 6 (2022): 1315–44.

[9] Florian Berg, "Why Do ESG Ratings Vary So Widely—and How Can Investors Make Sense of Them?," *Wall Street Journal*, November 2, 2022.

Chapter 16

[1] A couple of recent books also make the point that corporations are pursuing progressive political policies. Stephen R. Soukup, *The Dictatorship of Woke Capital: How Political Correctness Captured Big Business* (New York: Encounter Books, 2021); and Vivek Ramaswamy, *Woke, Inc. Inside Corporate America's Social Justice Scam* (New York: Hachette, 2021).

[2] Kate Gibson, "These Companies Are Paying for Abortion Travel," CBS News, July 2, 2022.

[3] All these corporations were Human Rights Campaign "Platinum Partners" in 2022, https://www.hrc.org/corporate-downloads/partners.

[4] Human Rights Campaign, "Human Rights Campaign Endorses Vice President Joe Biden for President," Human Rights Campaign News, May 6, 2020.

[5] Civic Alliance, "The Right to Vote is the Cornerstone of our Democracy," April 2, 2021.

[6] United Airlines, Twitter, April 6, 2021, 9:30 a.m., https://twitter.com/united/status/1379426304857141250?lang=en.

[7] John Kass, "Column: What Was Marx's Position on High-End Real Estate? Ask BLM's Patrisse Khan-Cullors," *Chicago Tribune*, April 15, 2021.

[8] Andrew Kerr, "Major Corporate Donors Silent on Black Lives Matter's Alleged Self-Dealing," *Washington Examiner*, June 3, 2022.

[9] For example, every Republican senator and two Democratic senators, West Virginia Sen. Joe Manchin and Montana Sen. Jon Tester, voted against a Biden administration regulation that would allow retirement-plan fund managers to consider climate change and other ESG factors when making investment decisions. See Andre Ackerman and Lindsay Wise, "Senate Votes 50–46 to Reverse ESG Rule for Retirement Funds," *Wall Street Journal*, March 1, 2023.

[10] Net Zero Asset Managers initiative, website.

[11] Net Zero Asset Managers initiative, website.

[12] Climate Action 100+, website.

[13] Climate Action 100+, website.

[14] ClimateWatch, Net-Zero Tracker, website.

[15] "Dallas Fed Energy Survey," Federal Reserve Bank of Dallas, March 23, 2022.

[16] "Dallas Fed Energy Survey," Federal Reserve Bank of Dallas, June 23, 2021.

[17] Net-Zero Banking Alliance, UN-Convened Environment Programme Initiative, home page.

[18] Net-Zero Banking Alliance, Commitment Statement.

[19] Consumers' Research, "Anti-ESG Actions and Legislation Tracker."

[20] Mark Brnovich and Doug Peterson, letter from the Arizona and Nebraska state attorneys general and others to Laurence D. Fink, CEO, BlackRock, August 4, 2022.

[21] Ross Kerber, "Eighteen U.S. States Join Missouri Probe into Morningstar ESG," Reuters, August 17, 2022.

[22] Lydia Saad and Jeffrey M. Jones, "What Percentage of Americans Own Stocks?," Gallup, May 12, 2022.

Chapter 17

[1] Alina Polianskaya, "Humans May Have Been Trading with Each Other as Far Back as 300,000 Years," *inews*, March 15, 2018.

[2] Oliver Hart and Luigi Zingales, "Companies Should Maximize Shareholder Welfare Not Market Value," *Journal of Law, Finance, and Accounting* 2 (2017): 247–274.

[3] "The State of Small Business Now," U.S. Chamber of Commerce, April 10, 2023.

[4] See the United States section of "Listed Domestic Companies, Total," World Federation of Exchanges database, World Bank.

[5] Steven Eder, "When Picking Apples on a Farm with 5,000 Rules, Watch Out for the Ladder," *New York Times*, December 27, 2017.

[6] Regulation statistics are provided by QuantGov, Mercatus Center at George Mason University, Arlington, VA: https://www.quantgov.org/state-regdata-definitive-edition.

[7] QuantGov, Mercatus Center.

[8] QuantGov, Mercatus Center.

[9] Agency regulatory statistics are provided by QuantGov, Mercatus Center at George Mason University, Arlington, VA: https://www.quantgov.org/agency-restrictions.

[10] At the end of 2008, there were 144,788 EPA regulations. At the end of 2012, there were 161,371. Agency regulatory statistics, QuantGov, Mercatus Center, https://www.quantgov.org/agency-restrictions.

[11] Nadja Popovich, Livia Albeck-Ripka, and Kendra Pierre-Louis, "The Trump Administration Rolled Back More Than 100 Environmental Rules. Here's the Full List," *New York Times,* January 20, 2021.

[12] "Tracking Regulatory Changes in the Biden Era," Brookings Center on Regulations and Markets.

[13] Emily Ekins, "68% of Americans Wouldn't Pay $10 a Month in Higher Electric Bills to Combat Climate Change," *Cato at Liberty* (blog), March 8, 2019.

[14] Liz Hamel et al., "The Kaiser Family Foundation/Washington Post Climate Change Survey," Kaiser Family Foundation, November 27, 2019.

[15] Wei Peng et al., "The Surprisingly Inexpensive Cost of State-Driven Emission Control Strategies," *Nature Climate Change* 11, no. 9 (2021): 738–45. See also Bjorn Lomborg, "Biden's Climate Ambitions Are Too Costly for Voters," *Wall Street Journal*, October 14, 2021.

[16] "Zero Carbon Bill Economic Analysis: A Synthesis of Economic Impacts" Ministry for the Environment, New Zealand Government, 2018, p. 20.

[17] Lomborg, "Biden's Climate Ambitions."

[18] Ove Hoegh-Guldberg et al., "Impacts of 1.5°C Global Warming on Natural and Human Systems," in *Global Warming of 1.5°C*, ed. V. Masson-Delmotte et al. (Cambridge, UK: Cambridge University Press, 2018), pp. 175–312.

[19] A recent report by the Biden Administration summarized 12 peer-reviewed studies and the consensus estimate is about 2 percent. Perhaps the actual cost will be much higher. My point is not to argue about what the future will be. Rather, my point is that it is not unreasonable to base policy on an estimate of around 2 percent. Council of Economic Advisors and Office of Management and Budget, "Methodologies and Considerations for Integrating the Physical and Transition Risks of Climate Change Into Macroeconomic Forecasting for the President's Budget," White Paper, March 13, 2023; and Richard G. Newell, Brian C. Prest, and Steven E. Sexton, "The GDP-Temperature Relationship: Implications for Climate Change Damages," *Journal of Environmental Economics and Management* 108 (2021): 102445.

[20] William Nordhaus, "Projections and Uncertainties about Climate Change in an Era of Minimal Climate Policies," *American Economic Journal: Economic Policy* 10, no. 3 (2018): 333–60.

[21] In Table 3 of Nordhaus, "Projections and Uncertainties," the DICE model estimate is 3.8 percent of GDP, which is 46 percent more than the UN's estimate of 2.6 percent.

[22] Bjorn Lomborg, "A Reasonable Alternative to COP26 and Preaching Climate Doom," *Wall Street Journal*, November 10, 2021.

[23] I am grateful to Alex Edmans for suggesting that I make this point.

[24] Lydia Saad and Jeffrey M. Jones, "What Percentage of Americans Own Stocks?," Gallup, May 12, 2022.

[25] Bruce Yandle, "Bootleggers and Baptists: The Education of a Regulatory Economist," *Regulation* 7 (1983): 12.

Chapter 18

[1] International Monetary Fund, "Views & Comments: McNamara on Population," *Finance & Development* 14, no. 2 (June 1977).

[2] Michael J. Cooper, Orlin Dimitrov, and P. Raghavendra Rau, "A Rose.com by Any Other Name," *Journal of Finance* 56, no. 6 (2001): 2371–88.

[3] Charles Mann, "The Book That Incited a Worldwide Fear of Overpopulation," *Smithsonian Magazine*, January 2018.

[4] Mann, "The Book That Incited a Worldwide Fear."

[5] Mann, "The Book That Incited a Worldwide Fear."

[6] Chelsea Follett, "The Cruel Truth about Population Control," *National Interest*, June 13, 2019.

[7] Follett, "The Cruel Truth."

[8] Chelsea Follett, "Neo-Malthusianism and Coercive Population Control in China and India: Overpopulation Concerns Often Result in Coercion" (Cato Institute Policy Analysis no. 897, July 21, 2020).

[9] Mann, "The Book That Incited a Worldwide Fear."

[10] Follett, "Neo-Malthusianism."

[11] My wife grew up in Harbin, China. She has relatives who were given such choices.

[12] Susan Greenhalgh, "Missile Science, Population Science: The Origins of China's One-Child Policy," *China Quarterly* 182 (2005): 253–76.

[13] United Nations Population Fund, United Nations Population Award.

[14] Follett, "Neo-Malthusianism."

[15] United Nations Population Fund, Background Document on the Population Programme of the UN, ICPD Library Resource, March 1994.

[16] Robert Zubrin, "The Population Control Holocaust," *New Atlantis*, no. 35 (Spring 2012): 33–54.

[17] Zubrin, "The Population Control Holocaust."

[18] Zubrin, "The Population Control Holocaust."

[19] Zubrin, "The Population Control Holocaust."

[20] Follett, "The Cruel Truth."

[21] Zubrin, CThe Population Control Holocaust."

[22] A year-by-year history of the WEF is available here: https://widgets.weforum.org/history/1973.html.

[23] Donella H. Meadows et al., *The Limits to Growth: The 30-Year Update* (New York: Basic Books, 1972).

[24] Thomas Malthus, *An Essay on the Principle of Population* (London: J. Johnson, 1798).

[25] Giovanni Federico and Antonio Tena Junguito, "How Many People on Earth? World Population 1800-1938," VoxEU, February 20, 2023.

[26] "Population, Total," World Bank data.

[27] GDP per capita data can be found on the World Bank's website: https://data.worldbank.org/indicator/NY.GDP.PCAP.CD.

[28] "Share of Population Living in Extreme Poverty, World, 1820 to 2018," Our World in Data.

[29] Ceri Parker, "The World Economic Forum at 50: A Timeline of Highlights from Davos and Beyond," World Economic Forum, December 20, 2019.

[30] Victoria Masterson, "Degrowth: What's behind the Economic Theory and Why Does It Matter Right Now?" World Economic Forum, June 15, 2022.

[31] Paul R. Ehrlich, Anne H. Ehrlich, and John P. Holdren, *Ecoscience: Population, Resources, Environment* (San Francisco: W. H. Freeman & Co., 1977).

[32] Ehrlich, Ehrlich, and Holdren, *Ecoscience.*

[33] Ehrlich, Ehrlich, and Holdren, *Ecoscience.*

[34] Paul Ehrlich, *The Population Bomb* (New York: Ballantine Books, 1968).

[35] Mark Perry, "18 Spectacularly Wrong Predictions Made around the Time of the First Earth Day in 1970, Expect More This Year," American Enterprise Institute, April 22, 2020.

[36] Paul Sabin, *The Bet: Paul Ehrlich, Julian Simon, and Our Gamble over Earth's Future* (New Haven, CT: Yale University Press, 2013).

[37] Darryl James, "Simon Says: Meet the Smith School Economist Who Took on the Doomsayers and Won," Robert H. Smith School of Business, University of Maryland, January 13, 2016.

[38] Sabin, *The Bet*.

[39] The 1980–2018 statistics are found on the Simon Abundance Index, "Time Price," at HumanProgress.org: https://www.humanprogress.org/simonproject/.

[40] John P. Holdren, Gretchen C. Daily, and Paul R. Ehrlich, "The Meaning of Sustainability: Biogeophysical Aspects," in *Defining and Measuring Sustainability: The Biogeophysical Foundations*, ed. Mohan Munasinghe and Walter Shearer (Washington: World Bank, 1995), pp. 3–17.

[41] Paul R. Ehrlich, MacArthur Fellows Program, MacArthur Foundation, August 1, 1990.

[42] Elizabeth Pollman, "The Origins and Consequences of the ESG Moniker," Institute for Law and Economics Research Paper No. 22–23, 2022.

[43] Principles for Responsible Investment, "What Are the Principles for Responsible Investment?"

[44] World Bank, "Sovereign ESG Data Framework, https://esgdata.worldbank.org/. See also: World Bank, "Global Program on Sustainability: Overview."

[45] Ray Cordato, "Obama's Green Energy Failure List," John Locke Foundation, October 30, 2012.

[46] More than 3,500 economists, including 28 Nobel Laureate economists, signed a statement of policy recommendations about global climate change. See "Economists' Statement on Carbon Dividends: Organized by the Climate Leadership Council."

[47] A classic bankruptcy risk measure is Altman's z-score. Edward I. Altman, "Financial Ratios, Discriminant Analysis and the Prediction of Corporate Bankruptcy," *Journal of Finance* 23, no. 4 (1968): 589–609. Ohlson's O-Score is another: James A. Ohlson, "Financial Ratios and the Probabilistic Prediction of Bankruptcy," *Journal of Accounting Research* (1980): 109–31.

[48] Florian Habermann and Felix Bernhard Fischer, "Corporate Social Performance and the Likelihood of Bankruptcy: Evidence from a Period of Economic Upswing," *Journal of Business Ethics* 182, no. 1 (2023): 243–59.

[49] David Deutsch, *The Beginning of Infinity* (London: Penguin Books, 2011), p. 436.

[50] Julian Simon made this point more than 40 years ago. Julian Simon, "And Now, the Good News: Life on Earth Is Improving," *Washington Post*, July 13, 1980.

[51] Paul M. Romer, "The Deep Structure of Economic Growth," PaulRomer.net, February 5, 2019.

Conclusion

[1] Joseph A. Schumpeter, *Capitalism, Socialism and Democracy* (New York: Harper & Brothers, 1942).

[2] Gregory Clark, *A Farewell to Alms* (Princeton, NJ: Princeton University Press, 2007).

[3] Max Roser et al., "Economic Growth," Our World in Data. In particular, the graph titled "Gross domestic product (GDP) by world region" shows that "Western Offshoots" (United States, Canada, New Zealand, and Australia) had GDP per capita growth of 21-fold during this period.

[4] J. Bradford DeLong, *Slouching towards Utopia: The Economic History of the Twentieth Century* (London: Profile Books, 2020).

INDEX

Note: Information in figures and tables is indicated by *f* or *t*; *n* designates a numbered note.

ABOUT THE AUTHOR

David McLean is the William G. Droms Professor of Finance at the McDonough School of Business at Georgetown University and the finance area chair. He has published widely on the topics of market efficiency, stock return predictability, and the interplay between financial markets and corporate investment.

ABOUT THE CATO INSTITUTE

Founded in 1977, the Cato Institute is a public policy research foundation dedicated to broadening the parameters of policy debate to allow consideration of more options that are consistent with the principles of limited government, individual liberty, and peace. To that end, the Institute strives to achieve greater involvement of the intelligent, concerned lay public in questions of policy and the proper role of government.

The Institute is named for *Cato's Letters*, libertarian pamphlets that were widely read in the American Colonies in the early 18th century and played a major role in laying the philosophical foundation for the American Revolution.

Despite the achievement of the nation's Founders, today virtually no aspect of life is free from government encroachment. A pervasive intolerance for individual rights is shown by government's arbitrary intrusions into private economic transactions and its disregard for civil liberties. And while freedom around the globe has notably increased in the past several decades, many countries have moved in the opposite direction, and most governments still do not respect or safeguard the wide range of civil and economic liberties.

To address those issues, the Cato Institute undertakes an extensive publications program on the complete spectrum of policy issues. Books, monographs, and shorter studies are commissioned to examine the federal budget, Social Security, regulation, military spending, international trade, and myriad other issues.

In order to maintain its independence, the Cato Institute accepts no government funding. Contributions are received from foundations, corporations, and individuals, and other revenue is generated from the sale of publications. The Institute is a nonprofit, tax-exempt, educational foundation under Section 501(c)3 of the Internal Revenue Code.

CATO INSTITUTE
1000 Massachusetts Ave. NW
Washington, DC 20001
www.cato.org

www.ingramcontent.com/pod-product-compliance
Lightning Source LLC
Chambersburg PA
CBHW022054210326
41519CB00054B/403